本书出版受贵州财经大学学科建设基金资助

王天剑　段　平◎编著

语言焦虑及其对策

Language Anxiety and Its Coping Strategies

中国社会科学出版社

图书在版编目(CIP)数据

语言焦虑及其对策 / 王天剑，段平编著 . —北京：中国社会科学出版社，2021.6

ISBN 978-7-5203-8123-9

Ⅰ.①语… Ⅱ.①王…②段… Ⅲ.①语言学习—研究 Ⅳ.①H09

中国版本图书馆 CIP 数据核字(2021)第 047048 号

出 版 人	赵剑英
责任编辑	周怡冰　刁佳慧
责任校对	韩天炜
责任印制	郝美娜

出　　版	中国社会科学出版社
社　　址	北京鼓楼西大街甲 158 号
邮　　编	100720
网　　址	http://www.csspw.cn
发 行 部	010-84083685
门 市 部	010-84029450
经　　销	新华书店及其他书店
印刷装订	北京君升印刷有限公司
版　　次	2021 年 6 月第 1 版
印　　次	2021 年 6 月第 1 次印刷
开　　本	710×1000　1/16
印　　张	12.5
插　　页	2
字　　数	205 千字
定　　价	85.00 元

凡购买中国社会科学出版社图书，如有质量问题请与本社营销中心联系调换
电话：010-84083683
版权所有　侵权必究

Preface

Language learning is not only influenced by cognitive factors, but also by non-cognitive factors. Anxiety is a non-cognitive factor defined as the fear or apprehension indirectly related to an object. Language anxiety is evoked by the learning or using of a language, especially a foreign or second language. It is very common among language learners of all ages.

The formal study of language anxiety began in 1940s. Early research showed confusing findings on the relationships between language learning and anxiety. Since the appearance of standardized research instruments in 1980s, research findings have tended to be consistent. Anxiety has generally been shown to be a destructive phenomenon in the course of language acquisition. It can be induced by the speaking, listening, reading or writing of a new language. Many variables have been found to be related to language anxiety. Those variables seem to constitute a hierarchy and influence the level of anxiety an individual may have.

Though numerous problems have been answered by research so far, more issues have been put forward. Further explorations are still in urgent need to gain a deeper understanding of the psychological mechanism of language anxiety, and to seek effective means to deal with the problem.

Based on the author's Ph. D. thesis abroad as well as recent years of research, this book provides a comprehensive discussion of the fundamental views and findings on language anxiety, such as the concept and identification of language anxiety, and the relationships of language anxiety to other variables involved in learning.

The anxiety coping strategies introduced in the book are primarily derived from psychotherapies (emotion regulation strategies), most of which are popular in clinics and counseling institutes for coping with social anxiety and various other mental disorders. Research in applied linguistics has provided evidences that those strategies are applicable to language anxiety. Needless to say, language anxiety is different from general social anxiety. Adaptation and development are indispensable for the successful transplant of general psychotherapies into the field of language education. Though the author has taken pains in the process of adaptation of the techniques, further improvement and modification are still required.

Due to the level of the author, there must be flaws and errors either in the content or in the language of the book. With all sincerity, the author hopes to get kind feedback from dear readers for future improvement of his work.

Contents

Chapter 1 Introduction ……………………………………… (1)
  1.1 Background ……………………………………………… (1)
  1.2 Outline of this book …………………………………… (3)
  1.3 Summary in Chinese …………………………………… (3)

Chapter 2 Language anxiety: Fundamental views and findings ………………………………… (5)
  2.1 Concept of anxiety ……………………………………… (5)
  2.2 Concept of language anxiety …………………………… (8)
  2.3 Identification of language anxiety …………………… (11)
  2.4 Relationships of language anxiety to learner variables ………… (12)
  2.5 Relationships of language anxiety to achievement and speaking ……………………………… (16)
  2.6 Theories on the roles of language anxiety …………… (18)
  2.7 Summary in Chinese …………………………………… (21)

Chapter 3 Teaching strategies for coping with language anxiety ………………………………… (23)
  3.1 Following the principles of connectionism …………… (23)
  3.2 Following the principles of constructivism …………… (25)
  3.3 Following the principles of transformative learning … (25)
  3.4 Following the principles of ACPO Model ……………… (26)
  3.5 Other recommendations ………………………………… (27)
  3.6 Summary in Chinese …………………………………… (28)

Chapter 4 Relaxation techniques for coping with language anxiety ……………………………… (30)
  4.1 Progressive muscle relaxation ………………………… (30)

4.2　Diaphragm breathing ············· (39)

4.3　Autogenic training ············· (40)

4.4　Guided imagery ············· (42)

4.5　Mindfulness meditation ············· (44)

4.6　Other relaxation related techniques ············· (46)

4.7　Summary in Chinese ············· (48)

Chapter 5　Systematic desensitization and cognitive behavioral therapies for language anxiety ············· (49)

5.1　Systematic desensitization ············· (49)

5.2　Cognitive behavioral therapies ············· (53)

5.3　Summary in Chinese ············· (63)

Chapter 6　Design of a psychoeducation lecture for language anxiety ············· (64)

6.1　Rationale and components of the psychoeducation lecture ········· (64)

6.2　Script of the psychoeducation lecture ············· (67)

6.3　Summary in Chinese ············· (87)

Chapter 7　Study of the effect of psychoeducation lecture on speaking anxiety ············· (88)

7.1　Methodology ············· (88)

7.2　Data analysis and results ············· (112)

7.3　Discussion ············· (126)

7.4　Conclusion and pedagogical implications ············· (133)

7.5　Summary in Chinese ············· (137)

Chapter 8　Findings on emotion regulation strategies for language anxiety ············· (138)

8.1　Relaxation oriented emotion regulation strategies ············· (138)

8.2　Cognition and behavior oriented emotion regulation strategies ············· (143)

8.3　Summary in Chinese ············· (143)

Bibliography ············· (145)

Appendixes .... (158)

Appendix A　Speaking Anxiety Scale .... (158)

Appendix B　Questionnaire on Disposition and Learning .... (160)

Appendix C　Speaking State Anxiety Scale .... (166)

Appendix D　Speaking Performance Assessment Criteria .... (167)

Appendix E　Invitation Letter .... (169)

Appendix F　Chinese Script of the Psychoeducation Lecture .... (170)

Appendix G　Distribution of Selections on the Likert Scales .... (183)

中文目录

第1章 引言 …………………………………………… (1)
1.1 背景 ………………………………………………… (1)
1.2 本书结构 …………………………………………… (3)
1.3 中文小结 …………………………………………… (3)
第2章 语言焦虑：基本观点和研究发现 ……………… (5)
2.1 焦虑的概念 ………………………………………… (5)
2.2 语言焦虑的概念 …………………………………… (8)
2.3 语言焦虑的识别 …………………………………… (11)
2.4 语言焦虑与学习者变量的关系 …………………… (12)
2.5 语言焦虑与语言成就和口语表达的关系 ………… (16)
2.6 关于语言焦虑影响的理论 ………………………… (18)
2.7 中文小结 …………………………………………… (21)
第3章 应对语言焦虑的教学策略 ……………………… (23)
3.1 遵循联想主义原则 ………………………………… (23)
3.2 遵循建构主义原则 ………………………………… (25)
3.3 遵循转换学习原则 ………………………………… (25)
3.4 遵循 ACPO 模型原则 ……………………………… (26)
3.5 其他教学建议 ……………………………………… (27)
3.6 中文小结 …………………………………………… (28)
第4章 应对语言焦虑的放松技巧 ……………………… (30)
4.1 渐进性肌肉放松 …………………………………… (30)
4.2 腹式呼吸 …………………………………………… (39)
4.3 自律训练 …………………………………………… (40)
4.4 意象引导 …………………………………………… (42)
4.5 正念冥想 …………………………………………… (44)

4.6　其他放松技术 ……………………………………… (46)
4.7　中文小结 …………………………………………… (48)
第5章　语言焦虑的系统脱敏与认知行为疗法 ………… (49)
5.1　系统脱敏 …………………………………………… (49)
5.2　认知行为疗法 ……………………………………… (53)
5.3　中文小结 …………………………………………… (63)
第6章　应对语言焦虑的心理教育讲座设计 …………… (64)
6.1　心理教育讲座的基本原理和组成部分 …………… (64)
6.2　心理教育讲座的脚本 ……………………………… (67)
6.3　中文小结 …………………………………………… (87)
第7章　心理教育讲座影响口语焦虑的实证研究 ……… (88)
7.1　方法 ………………………………………………… (88)
7.2　数据分析和结果 …………………………………… (112)
7.3　讨论 ………………………………………………… (126)
7.4　结论和教学意义 …………………………………… (133)
7.5　中文小结 …………………………………………… (137)
第8章　情绪调节策略影响语言焦虑的研究发现 ……… (138)
8.1　放松类情绪调节策略 ……………………………… (138)
8.2　认知和行为类情绪调节策略 ……………………… (143)
8.3　中文小结 …………………………………………… (143)
参考文献 …………………………………………………… (145)
附录 ………………………………………………………… (158)
附录A　口语焦虑量表 …………………………………… (158)
附录B　性格和学习调查问卷 …………………………… (160)
附录C　口语状态焦虑量表 ……………………………… (166)
附录D　口语评定标准 …………………………………… (167)
附录E　邀请函 …………………………………………… (169)
附录F　心理教育讲座的中文脚本 ……………………… (170)
附录G　李克特量表上的选择分布 ……………………… (183)

Chapter 1　Introduction

1.1　Background

"My heart beats fast when I'm asked to speak English in the class!"

"I'm overwhelmed by the complicated rules I have to learn before I can use a second language."

"I tend to sleep badly before a language test."

"I made so many mistakes because I was extremely nervous."

"I try to avoid eye contact with the language teacher whenever he decides to ask one of us to answer a question."

Talks as such are familiar to language teachers. They are all symptoms of language anxiety, the fear and apprehension involved in language learning or using. Due to its importance in learning as well as performance, language anxiety draws a great deal of attention from researchers. Efforts to cope with the problem of language anxiety create a new field of study.

Academic interests in the connection between anxiety and second language learning started in the 1940s. Early investigation produced confusing findings. Some studies displayed positive correlations of anxiety with language proficiency, while others exposed negative ones. Moreover, there were explorations which discovered no correlations (Scovel, 1978). The confusing discoveries made researchers incapable of creating a clear picture about how anxiety influences language acquisition and performance. Examining the literature that was available then, Scovel (1978) arrived at the conclusion that it was hard to decide the impacts of language anxiety on learning due to: (a) the discrepancy of instruments employed to measure anxiety, and (b) the intricate and complicated hierarchy of factors that may interfere in the course of language learning.

Scovel recommended that researchers needed to notice the different sorts of anxiety which had been recognized, and be accurate about the kind of anxiety involved in their measurement. MacIntyre & Gardner (1991c) proposed that three sorts of anxiety—the trait, the state, and the situation-specific anxiety—might be recognized in research on the roles played by anxiety in second language acquisition. Horwitz, and Cope (1986) suggested that the anxiety which was responsible for learners' harmful emotional responses to language learning was the situation-specific anxiety. They termed it Foreign Language Anxiety, and created a tool, the Foreign Language Classroom Anxiety Scale (FLCAS), to assess this anxiety. Based on the findings of Horwitz et al., the instrument had a high internal consistency, obtaining an alpha coefficient of .93. A test-retest method spanning eight weeks achieved a reliability of $r = .83$ ($p < .001$). In a study of construct validity, it was revealed that the FLCAS correlated with but was different from other sorts of anxiety.

The situation-specific point of view on anxiety explains many earlier bewildering findings. Horwitz (2001) examined relevant literature and recommended that studies employing the FLCAS and other exact measures of language anxiety had revealed consistent modest negative correlations between anxiety and language proficiency (normally final grades).

Aside from the relationship of language anxiety to achievement, numerous studies have also explored the relationships of anxiety to other variables. It has been shown that language anxiety is connected with plenty of learner variables (e.g., gender, age, learning experience, character, aptitude for language, proficiency, motivation and cultural factors). It is also associated with the task variables (e.g., listening, reading, speaking, and writing). The approaches to teaching and the beliefs of language teachers can also produce an influence on language anxiety. Our understanding about the connection between language anxiety and these factors is still pretty inadequate. We can not come to conclusions on many issues. There are a lot of disputes among researchers on many basic problems. For instance, researchers can not arrive at agreement about if language anxiety plays mainly a causal or "side effect" role in the course of second language acquisition (MacIntyre, 1995; Sparks & Ganschow, 2007; Horwitz, 2001). Moreover, few studies have tried to investigate therapies for language anxiety.

All the problems suggest that more research should be given to the topic of language anxiety.

1.2 Outline of this book

The present book provides a general discussion and description of the fundamental views and findings on language anxiety, the techniques for the control of this emotional problem, and the central section of the author's PhD degree work.

The book is divided into 8 chapters. Chapter 1, the present part, is a brief introduction. Chapter 2 focuses on the concept about language anxiety, findings on the relationships of language anxiety to learner and learning variables, and relevant theories on language anxiety. Chapter 3 discusses teaching strategies. Chapters 4 to 6 are about emotion regulation strategies. Chapter 4 introduces several relaxation exercises, Chapter 5 is on systematic desensitization and cognitive behavioral therapy, and Chapter 6 presents the design of a psychoeducation lecture for coping with language anxiety. Chapter 7 is a study of the effect of the psychoeducation lecture on language anxiety. Chapter 8, the last section, provides a review of the findings of studies on emotion regulation strategies.

1.3 Summary in Chinese

针对焦虑与二语学习关系的研究始于20世纪40年代。早期研究结果分歧较大：有人发现焦虑与语言学习呈负相关，有人发现两者呈正相关，还有人发现两者无显著相关。随着人们对语言焦虑概念认识的统一，以及测量工具的标准化，研究结果逐渐趋向一致：语言焦虑与语言学习呈负相关。

本书围绕语言焦虑及其对策展开，内容分为八章。第一章为本书引言。第二章聚焦于语言焦虑的概念、语言焦虑与学习者变量的关系及其影响学习的理论解释。第三章至第六章是关于语言焦虑的可选对策。其中第三章讨论了教学策略；第四章介绍了几种放松训练；第五章阐释了系统去敏和认知行为疗法；第六章是一个基于理性情绪行为疗法的心理教育讲座设计。第七章呈现的是检验心理教育讲座有效性的实证研究。第八章是关于不同情感管理策略的研究发现。

Chapter 2　Language anxiety: Fundamental views and findings

Being an emotional response in learning, language anxiety attracts a lot of interest from researchers and educators due to the crucial roles it plays in the acquisition of a language. This chapter focuses on the fundamental views and findings accumulated up to now. It begins with a discussion of the concepts of general anxiety and language anxiety, and continues with an introduction of the techniques for identifying language anxiety. Subsequently, literature on the relationships of language anxiety to learner variables and language learning/ using are covered.

2.1　Concept of anxiety

(1) Divergent definitions

Language anxiety is a specific type of anxiety. To achieve a full understanding of language anxiety, it is essential to begin with general anxiety. The term anxiety has been defined from several perspectives by experts in different fields of study, such as psychology, pathology and anthropology:

Darwin (1872) considered anxiety to be an emotional response which is provoked when an organism perceives physical threat;

May (1977) thought of anxiety to be an emotional reaction to threat to value which an individual regards as crucial to his personality;

Beck and his colleagues (Beck & Emery, 1985) proposed that anxiety is a type of emotional reaction resulting from a flawed perception of risk in an environment.

Those are merely a few instances of the different interpretations of the term anxiety. Being the Father of the Theory of Evolution, the scientist Darwin emphasized the adaptive role of anxiety, which helps an organism prepare for dealing with the physical threats he perceives. Anxiety therefore is favorable for surviving risky situations. This definition is imperfect because in modern society many people are still complaining about having anxiety although they are in situations that have no real physical threats. The definition offered by May can explain the type of anxiety without actual physical threat: what matters is the threat to people's value. But it is still not complete since it overlooks the fact that in a civilized society there still exist physically threatening events such as epidemics, earthquakes, wars or hurricanes which can cause anxiety. From a psychotherapist's perspective, Beck considered anxiety to be the consequence of defective cognition of a person, rather than that of reality. This concept of anxiety is validated by the successful experiences of psychotherapists who have effectively eliminated anxiety via helping clients alter their problematical thoughts. But the definition by Beck is still in question. The cognitions leading to the problem of anxiety are not always defective.

As is clear, those notions disagree on the triggers of anxiety. Each can enlighten some types of anxiety, but cannot explain others. Specifying the causes seems to be a drawback for defining the term of anxiety. Scovel (1978) avoided the issue by simply defining it as a state of apprehension, an unclear fear which is merely indirectly connected with an object. With no specification of the cause, the definition seems applicable to all categories of anxiety. That is probably the reason for this definition being widely cited by fellow researchers.

(2) Essential components

Generally speaking, typical anxiety has four essential components: the cognitive, the somatic, the emotional, and the behavioral components. They combine to produce a unique uncomfortable feeling of anxiety.

The cognitive part is the thoughts or beliefs associated with anxiety. It may be the anticipation of the advent of certain frightening events, the assessment of the possibility of the occurrence of unwelcome events, or the appraisal of the results of the events. Individuals in anxiety are prone to having faulty cognitions like overgeneralization, magnifying the probability, catastrophizing the consequence, and so forth.

The emotional component is the mental experience suffered by an individual in anxiety. Anxious people can experience nervousness, apprehension, irritability, dread, obsession, jumpiness, and so on.

The somatic element of anxiety denotes the part of physiological responses going with anxiety. They are related to the autonomous system. These symptoms vary a lot from person to person. They may probably be muscle tension, nausea, tenseness, headache, chest pain, stomachache, or shortness of breath, depending on the level of anxiety. The body is in a state of arousal for coping with a threat: the heartbeat is increased, the blood flows fast to the main muscle groups, and the work of the digestive and immune systems is inhibited (fight-or-flight reaction). External signs may include trembling, pale skin, and sweating face.

The behaviors selected by people in anxiety are the behavioral component. Confronting the threat directly, withdrawing from it, or doing something else are all possible choices. It has been found by researchers in social situations that anxious individuals stutter and stammer when they talk, squirm in their chairs, play with their clothes, hair or other objects, or fidget (Leary, 1982). They are also inclined to choose image-protection behaviors like restraining themselves from taking part in the conversation, always smiling or nodding, or seldom interrupting other people (Young, 1991).

(3) State and trait anxiety

The differentiation between state and trait anxiety was suggested by Spielberger (1983). State anxiety is a momentary subjective feeling of worry, tension, apprehension, and nervousness, accompanied by arousal of the person's nervous system. Trait anxiety is considered as a comparatively stable interpersonal difference in anxiety - tendency. Needless to say, the anxiety referred to in the previous sections is simply state anxiety. Academically speaking, trait anxiety is an attribute or trait. It is just a personal proneness to experiencing anxiety.

Spielberger (1983) created the State-Trait Anxiety Inventory (STAI) to investigate the two types of anxiety. This instrument is composed of a trait anxiety subscale and a state anxiety subscale. They both take the Likert format, and each is composed of 20 items. Each of the 20 items in the state anxiety subscale is followed by four items: (a) Very much so, (b) Moderately so, (c) Somewhat, and (d) Not at all. Each of the 20 items in the trait anxiety subscale is also followed by four choices: (a) Almost always, (b) Often, (c) Sometimes, and (d) Almost never. For the state anxiety subscale, the direction or instruction requires the subjects to provide selections according to the temporary emotions felt at the time of the anxiety test; for the trait anxiety subscale, the direction or instruction notifies the subjects to provide responses based on the emotional reactions usually experienced, not on those experienced at the time of the investigation. Displayed below are some sample items from each of the subscales:

State anxiety subscale
- I feel calm.

a) Very much so   b) Moderately so   c) Somewhat   d) Not at all
- I feel secure.

a) Very much so   b) Moderately so   c) Somewhat   d) Not at all
- I am tense.

a) Very much so   b) Moderately so   c) Somewhat   d) Not at all

Trait anxiety subscale
- I feel pleasant.

a) Almost always   b) Often   c) Sometimes   d) Almost never
- I feel satisfied with myself.

a) Almost always   b) Often   c) Sometimes   d) Almost never
- I feel rested.

a) Almost always   b) Often   c) Sometimes   d) Almost never

2.2 Concept of language anxiety

The notion of general anxiety, though helpful, is not sufficient for researcher in the study of second language acquisition. It can not clarify the confusing findings of early studies. There were studies revealing incomplete correlations of anxiety to language achievements. Swain and Burnaby (1976), for instance, examined English speaking French students, and found a negative correlation between one assessment of anxiety and French proficiency and no correlation between other assessments of anxiety and French proficiency. In the study by Tucker, Hamayan, & Genesee (1976), it was also revealed that anxiety has a significant correlation with one measure of French level, but no significant correlation with any of several other measures of French proficiency. There were also studies which found consistent correlations. But these correlations were not applicable to other students or languages. Take the study by Chastain (1975) for example. They found a significant negative correlation between anxiety and the test scores of French among students taught with audio-lingual method, and a significant positive correlation between anxiety and the test scores of German and Spanish among students taught with the traditional method.

Based on the impacts of anxiety on achievement, Alpert and Haber (1960) tried to explain the inconsistence with the concepts of debilitating and facilitating anxieties. They proposed that these variables were independent of each other. One may have debilitating anxiety, facilitating anxiety, both of them, or neither of them. According to Scovel (1978), facilitating anxiety could stimulate a learner to approach the learning task, but debilitating anxiety could spur a learner to avoid it. In the opinion of Chastain (1975), perhaps a low level of anxiety is helpful, while a high level of anxiety is destructive.

But these were merely assumptions unsatisfactory to other researchers. The confusing findings were partly due to the inconsistent instruments employed (Scovel, 1978). The different concepts of anxiety held by researchers were responsible for the inconsistency of instruments used. To clarify the embarrassing situation, it is necessary to introduce a clear and commonly accepted notion of anxiety related to language learning.

One definition of language anxiety is the feeling of apprehension and tension associated with second language situations, including listening, speaking and learning (MacIntyre and Gardner, 1994a). A more specific definition of language anxiety was given by Horwitz et al. (1986), who considered test anxiety, communication apprehension, and fear of negative evaluation as the components of foreign language anxiety. It is the fear of failure which features test anxiety. It belongs to a type of performance anxiety (Gordon & Sarason, as cited in Horwitz et al., 1991). Students suffering from test anxiety usually set excessively demanding standards for themselves. They become anxious when confronting a challenging test. Test-anxious students suffer a lot in foreign language class due to the frequent tests inherent in the learning. Fearing to communicate with people is responsible for communication apprehension. According to Horwitz et al. (1986), being incapable of expressing one's thoughts and ideas in a foreign language or being incapable of comprehending another person are potential causes of communication apprehension for language students. Fear of negative evaluation is the apprehension about appraisal from others. In fear of being negative evaluated, those learners tend to avoid evaluative situations (Watson & Friend, as cited in Horwitz et al., 1991). This type of language anxiety is different from fear of negative evaluation since it is not confined to test-taking situations.

Foreign language anxiety, according to Horwitz et al. (1986), is not simply the sum of test anxiety, communication apprehension, and fear of negative evaluation. It is a distinct complex of behaviors, self-perceptions, feelings, and beliefs arising from the context of classroom language learning.

Being a sort of situation-specific trait, foreign language anxiety is stable over time but confined to the particular contexts of language learning. The anxiety related to particular language skills, such as listening, writing, reading, and speaking are all situation specific anxieties, besides those specified by Horwitz et al. (1986). Differing from state anxiety, situation-specific anxiety is the tendency to experience anxiety, rather than the ongoing feeling of anxiety. Language anxiety is not to be confused with trait anxiety. It is a tendency limited to the language performance situations, rather than across all situations. In fact, situation-specific anxiety can be considered as trait anxiety in a given context (MacIntyre and Gardner, 1991a).

Observing and examining language anxiety as a situation-specific construct, researchers have since obtained relatively consistent findings on the impacts of language anxiety. Earlier confusing findings can thus be clarified.

2.3 Identification of language anxiety

In the foreign language classroom, learners having different levels of anxiety may have different characteristics, which can be identified. Basic means for the identification of language anxiety include observation and self-report (Scovel, as cited in Madsen, Brown, & Jones, 1991).

(1) Observation

Anxiety is related to an array of obvious symptoms and behaviors, such as facial expressions, gestures, postures, voices, and so on. These symptoms and behaviors can be observed by researchers and educators. Nevertheless, observation is not sensitive. Researchers can hardly distinguish between students with different levels of language anxiety. It is therefore not commonly used as a measure of language anxiety (Snyder & Ray, 1971).

(2) Self-report

The most widely used approaches for measuring language anxiety is self-report. Self-report methods usually take the forms of Likert scales. Subjects are required to select from the choices offered by the scale to convey their anxiety. The Foreign Language Classroom Anxiety Scale (FLCAS) by Horwitz et al. (1986) is a widely employed self-report Likert scales. Thirty-three items are covered by the FLCAS, and each item is expressed by a five-point sub-scale. The choices include: a) Strongly disagree, b) Disagree, c) Undecided, d) Agree, and e) Strongly agree. Here are a few sample items:

• I never feel quite sure of myself when I am speaking English in my foreign language class.

a) Strongly disagree b) Disagree c) Undecided d) Agree e) Strongly agree

• I am usually at ease during tests in my language class.

a) Strongly disagree b) Disagree c) Undecided d) Agree e) Strongly agree

• I am afraid that the other students will laugh at me when I speak the foreign language.

a) Strongly disagree b) Disagree c) Undecided d) Agree e) Strongly agree

Test anxiety, communication apprehension, and fear of negative evaluation are addressed by the items presented in FLCAS. The scale is highly valid and reliable. General language anxiety rather than state anxiety is tapped.

Marking on a linear figure expressing the continuity of the levels of anxiety is another self-report technique, which is less commonly employed (MacIntyre & Gardner, 1991b). Like a thermometer, this method is intuitive for showing the level of anxiety.

2.4 Relationships of language anxiety to learner variables

Learner variables refer to differences between groups of learners or individual learners. Only non-linguistic variables are covered in this section, which include culture, gender, personality, belief, and state anxiety. The relationships of language anxiety to language proficiency and performance are presented in a separate section.

(1) Culture and language anxiety

Horwitz (2001) noted comparatively different means of anxiety scores on the FLCAS in a study involving various cultural groups. Americans showed similar levels of language anxiety, Korean EFL learners displayed higher levels, and Turkish learners of English had lower levels. Based on the finding, Horwitz inferred language anxiety might differ between learners from different cultural groups. The English learners coming from Confucian Heritage Cultures (e.g., China, Japan and Korea) were found to have higher levels of language anxiety than those from Vietnam and Europe (Woodrow, 2006).

(2) Belief and language anxiety

A person's beliefs related to himself or language learning can also have some influence on language anxiety. The beliefs on oneself are termed self-constructs, which include self-confidence, self-efficacy, self-concept, and self-esteem (Mercer, 2008). It is supported by a great number of studies that self-constructs are correlated with language anxiety.

In a study by Kitano (2001), students' perceptions of their speaking ability in the language they were learning were measured by a self-rating scale, as well as a scale for self-rating of the native speakers' perception. The result showed that students' levels of language anxiety were negatively correlated with their improved perceptions of their own abilities. In the study by Gardner, Tremblay & Masgoret (1997), learners with higher confidence had a lower level of language anxiety and a higher level of proficiency, while those with lower confidence had a higher level of language anxiety and a lower level of proficiency. In the investigation by MacIntyre, Noels & Clément (1997), anxious students were found to be inclined to underrate their proficiency. It has also been found that low self-confidence is one of the components of FLCAS (Matsuda & Gobel, 2004). Previous studies support the judgment that self-construct and language anxiety are closely related.

Beliefs about learning a language are also revealed to be related to language anxiety. Young (1991) proposed six sources of language anxiety, one of which is learner beliefs about learning a language. Perfectionism has been noticed to be destructive. It was found that students' tendency to be perfectionistic had contributed to their levels of anxiety in language classes (Price, 1991). The test anxiety suffered by some students is also because of their perfectionism. Those students are habitually over-demanding on themselves and consider anything less than a perfect performance to be a failure on a test (Horwitz et al., 1986). According to Horwitz et al. (1991), anxious students are afraid that they could not understand all language input. Perfectionism is responsible for the fear of those learners.

Besides perfectionism, other inappropriate types of beliefs are also connected with language anxiety. Ohata (2005, p.7) provided an example that "if beginning learners believe that pronunciation is the single most important aspect of L2 learning, they would naturally get frustrated to find the reality of their imperfect speech even after a lot of practice". Horwitz et al. (1991) found that many students insisted that the second language should not be spoken until one could speak it correctly and that it was unacceptable to guess about unknown words. They proposed that such types of beliefs can result in anxiety since students have to use the second language in communication before they can speak it fluently and that guessing about unknown words are unavoidable even for excellent learners.

Since anxiety is closely related to beliefs, it is possible to cope with language anxiety via restructuring one's beliefs.

(3) Personality and language anxiety

The integrated pattern of emotions, behaviors and thoughts produces personality. This pattern distinguishes one person from another (Peng, 2001). Psychologists have advanced various theories on personality. Unwillingness to communicate and trait anxiety are to be discussed in this section. Both of them are typical features of personality, and have been found relevant to language anxiety.

a. Trait anxiety and language anxiety

In a study by Horwitz (1991), language anxiety was measured by the FLCAS, while trait anxiety was measured by the Trait Anxiety Inventory (Spielberger, 1983). The result showed that there was a significant positive correlation between the two variables.

b. Unwillingness to communicate and language anxiety

Burgoon (1976) discovered that learners having communication reticence showed the personality of unwillingness to communicate. Liu and Jackson (2008) discovered a moderate correlation between language anxiety and unwillingness to communicate.

(4) State anxiety and language anxiety

State anxiety is the temporary arousal of anxiety. Language anxiety, instead, is the general tendency to feel anxious in situations where foreign or second language is learnt or used. There is a close relationship between the two. According to MacIntyre and Gardner (1994a), students reporting having experienced language anxiety before are prone to suffering from state anxiety when they are exposed to the context of language class.

(5) Gender and language anxiety

Contradictory results have been yielded with regard to the relationship between gender and on language anxiety. Whether gender is connected to anxiety, and whether males or females are more prone to anxiety are still confusing.

In the study by Aida (1994) and Chang (1996), there was no differences in language anxiety in terms of gender. In the study by Matsuda & Gobel (2004), first - semester English students at a Japanese university were investigated. It was found that gender was not significantly related to general or reading anxieties, nor was it related to the subcomponents of either type of anxiety (e. g. , Low Speaking Self-Confidence, Reading Confidence, etc.).

Direct relationships between gender and anxiety were revealed by quite a few studies. The findings, however, were still incompatible. Males seemed to be more liable to anxiety in some of such studies. In the exploration by Kitano (2001), the college learners of Japanese were subjects. Anxiety was correlated with self-perception of ability among male students. They felt higher levels of anxiety when they believed that their spoken Japanese was less competent than their friends. Among female students, such an association was not observed. The researchers explained the male students' proneness to anxiety in terms of the learning context: perceiving language learning as a female major made men feel less comfortable. In the viewpoint of Onwuegbuzie, Bailey, and Daley (2001), a female oriented language learning culture might exist.

Females were found to be more liable to anxiety by other studies. Using Hispanic learners as subjects, Mejías, Applebaum, et al. (1991) discovered that females had higher anxiety than males. The finding is supported by Machida (2001), who reported that for learners of Japanese, females had higher anxiety than males. Elkhafaifi (2005) studied postsecondary learners of Arabic, and noticed that females were more anxious than males. But gender was not found to be related to anxiety in listening by the researcher. In a longitudinal study, MacIntyre, Baker, et al. (2002) discovered that boys' levels of anxiety remained constant from the 7th to the 9th grade, although girls showed a reduction in anxiety from the 8th to the 9th grade.

Various factors may be responsible for the inconsistent findings, and further exploration is still in need.

2.5 Relationships of language anxiety to achievement and speaking

Most language teachers and researchers are concerned with the connection between language anxiety and leaning. Learning is typically reflected by the overall achievement and specific language skills. The following sections focus on how language anxiety is related to the overall achievement and the skill of speaking.

2.5.1 Overall achievement and language anxiety

A range of criteria have been employed as indexes of achievement. Experts usually use course grades, scores of self-reported proficiency, or scores of proficiency test as indexes of language achievement. Among various levels of learners, it has been found that language anxiety is negatively correlated with language achievement.

Using final scores as indicators of achievement, Chan & Wu (2004) found that language achievement was negatively correlated with language anxiety among elementary school EFL learners. Elkhafaifi (2005) discovered that the language anxiety of postsecondary students of Arabic was negatively correlated with the achievement. Wei (2007) found a significant negative correlation between self-reported proficiency and language anxiety in the study of undergraduate learners of English. Exploring the levels of anxiety among Chinese undergraduates of different proficiency levels, Liu (2006) reported that the more successful learners tended to show lower levels of anxiety. MacIntyre et al. (1997) found that language anxiety was robustly and negatively correlated with language competence for bilingual students at the university level.

Taking a situation specific view of anxiety, the studies mentioned above have all produced comparatively consistent results about the relationships between language achievement and anxiety. Those findings strongly support the claim by Horwitz (2001) about how language anxiety is related to language achievement.

2.5.2 Speaking and language anxiety

The anxiety connected with speaking performance in the second or foreign language is called speaking anxiety. It is supposed that speaking anxiety is the result of speaking. It also has a strong impact on speaking performance.

According to MacIntyre (1999), speaking is the most important cause of language anxiety. It has been found that students feel most anxious as they respond to their language teacher or are invited to speak English in the classroom (Liu, 2006). Because speaking is the most important source of anxiety for many students (Cheng, Horwitz, et al., 1999), the instruments for measuring general language anxiety usually have an overwhelming number of items addressing speaking. The strategies employed by students in communication and the quality of speech can both be influenced by speaking anxiety. To examine the effect of anxiety on oral performance, Steinberg and Horwitz (1986) conduced an experiment, in which anxiety was induced by a video camera, stress-loaded instructions, and cold manners of the examiners. When required to describe pictures of ambiguous scenes, the subjects experiencing anxiety evoking conditions were found to be less interpretive (more concrete) than the subjects undergoing relaxing conditions. In the study by Djigunović (2006), high anxiety language users made more false starts, used fewer repetitions, had longer pauses in a clause, and produced shorter continuous speeches in picture description tasks. Tiono & Sylvia (2004) reported that students having high communication apprehension were inclined to use repetition in picture description tasks. They needed more time for thinking. Students having low communication apprehension employed more approximation strategy. This indicated that they were bold enough to risk saying things which were close to their intentions. Liu and Jackson (2008) found that language anxiety was negatively and significantly correlated with language class risk-taking and language class sociability. Students having a higher level of anxiety seemed to have a lower motivation to use the language for the purpose of sociability, or to make use of forms beyond their sureness of correct use. MacIntyre and Gardner (1994b) noticed that students in higher anxiety provided shorter self-descriptions, which were judged as poorer in sentence complexity, lower in fluency, and less standard in accent.

Oral proficiency interview are likely to cause anxiety for the interviewee (Young, 1986). Although when ability was controlled, performance level was not found to be reduced by the increase of anxiety during the oral proficiency interview involved in her study, Young still believed oral proficiency interview could cause anxiety high enough to interfere with performance when it was actually used for grading or placement. The findings by Phillips (1992) was consistent with Young's belief. Phillips examined eight features of oral interview performance: (a) average length of Communication Units, (b) total number of words in Communication Units, (c) percent of correct Communication Units, (d) percent of words in correct Communication Units, (e) percent of words in mazes, (f) mean length of the mazes, (g) total number of target structures, and (h) total number of dependent clauses. The (b), (g), and (h) turned out to have significant correlations with language anxiety when the effect of ability was controlled. In a similar study, Wilson (2006) discovered that, with ability controlled, (b) and (e) had significant correlations with anxiety. Given the precise measurement and the control of ability, the findings reported by Phillips (1992) and Wilson (2006) concerning the relationship between anxiety and speaking performance were very convincing.

2.6 Theories on the roles of language anxiety

Because of the inconsistence of measurement, early research resulted in mixed findings on the role of anxiety in language learning and using. Findings have tended to converge with the conceptualization of language anxiety as a situation-specific construct, and the creation of corresponding instruments. Most studies yielded negative correlations between anxiety and language achievement. Because anxiety explorations generally use correlation to analyze the data, researchers cannot draw definite causal conclusions. Agreement has not been reached on whether language anxiety is mainly a result of poor learning, or a cause of poor learning.

2.6.1 Side-effect explanation of language anxiety

According to the linguistic coding deficit hypothesis (LCDH) by Sparks and Ganschow (1991, 1993a, 1993b), language aptitude is the main cause of individual differences in language achievement. As an affective variable, language anxiety seems to play the role of side effects.

The LCDH suggests that language system entails semantic, phonological, and syntactic codes. Difficulty in the learning of a second language results from one or more problem in these codes in the learner's mother tongue (Schwarz, 1997). This view closely associates the second language coding ability with the first (Zheng, 2008). The 10-year longitudinal study of fifty-four subjects by Sparks & Ganschow (2007) seems to support their suggestion. In the research, the subjects were tested using native language measures from first to fifth grades. The foreign language proficiency, language aptitude, and foreign language classroom anxiety of those subjects in high schools were also investigated. The proficiency and anxiety in the foreign language were found the to have a negative and significant correlation. There was a positive and significant correlation between foreign language proficiency and language aptitude. Native language measures, such as Test of Written Spelling and Test of Cognitive Skills, also had positive and significant correlations with language aptitude.

The roles played by affective variables like anxiety in language acquisition were discounted by Sparks and Ganschow. Their view was problematic, because it was based on a longitudinal survey, not on an experiment. It is vulnerable to draw a definite causal conclusion from a survey. The sample size of 54 subjects in their study was not large enough to be convincing. Their theory is incompatible with some other studies in which, with ability controlled, language performance was negatively affected by anxiety arousal.

2.6.2 Active-role explanations of language anxiety

More experts advocate the causal roles of anxiety in learning. In other words, those researchers stress the active-roles of language anxiety.

(1) Krashen's theory

According to the Affective Filter Hypothesis by Krashen (1982), learners having great self-confidence, high motivation, good self-image, and low levels of language anxiety have better chances to succeed in the acquisition of a second language. Learners with low self-esteem, low motivation, and high anxiety may suffer from increased affective filter, which reduces the efficiency of acquisition from comprehensible input.

(2) Baily's theory

According to Bailey's group dynamics theory (1983), competitive language learners tend to overtly compare their achievements or self-perceived achievements with the achievements of others or with their expectations. Once unsuccessful self images result from the comparisons, facilitating or debilitating anxiety may be provoked. Facilitating anxiety may increase learners' efforts at leaning, while debilitating anxiety may lead to decreased efforts at learning or avoidance of learning.

(3) Tobias's theory

Tobias (as cited in MacIntyre & Gardner, 1991a) suggested that an anxious person is inclined to focus on himself rather than on the task. These task-irrelevant thoughts compete with task-relevant ones for the limited cognitive resources. Non-anxious individuals have no such self-engagement, and gain an advantage when the task is hard. Distraction may occur at the input, output or processing stages, according to Tobias. In the phase of input, anxiety may result in poor initial processing of information. In the phase of output, anxiety may hinder the retrieval of information from the memory. In the phase of processing, anxiety may have little influence if the task is simple to the person, and have a great negative effect if the task is challenging to the person. This theory seems applicable to all types of anxiety, including language anxiety.

(4) Eysenck's theory

Eysenck (as cited from MacIntyre & Gardner, 1994b) provided an interpretation of the role of anxiety in terms of cognitive interference. According to his theory, the attention of anxious people is divided between self-related cognition and task-related cognition. The distraction of cognitive resources reduces the efficiency of performance. Anxious people may try to make up for their inefficiency by additional effort. If the additional effort is more than what is needed for the compensation, facilitating effect of anxiety may be observed. This theory also seems applicable to different types of anxiety.

All the theories mentioned above suggest that language anxiety plays an active role, which may be facilitative or debilitative. They seem to be complementary in nature. Krashen's view is related to language acquisition from comprehensible input. Bailey's view focuses on competitive learners. The views of Tobias and Eysenck have more to do with the cognitive interference of anxiety. According to McIntyre and Gardner (1994a), even when anxiety seems facilitative or at least not debilitative, it is not desirable. Anxious learners have been found to work harder than non-anxious learners, but their achievement is not in proportion to their effort (Horwitz et al., 1986; Price, 1991). Because debilitative anxiety may weaken the cognitive function, students in high anxiety may learn less or be incapable of demonstrating what they have acquired. As a consequence, they have a high probability of experiencing more frustrations, which may in turn increase their anxiety.

The disagreement on the role of anxiety in language learning is unlikely to be settled soon. A key factor responsible for the dispute is that most of the related studies are non-experimental. Probably a more helpful perspective to the topic is to stop arguing about the main role, and to accept findings on either side. Language anxiety can play the roles of cause and effect by turns. Reducing the learners' language anxiety seems desirable.

2.7 Summary in Chinese

焦虑是与目标间接相连的恐惧和紧张，它包含四个主成分：认知反应、身体反应、情绪反应和行为反应。焦虑分为特质焦虑和状态焦虑。语言焦虑是与语言学习和应用相关的焦虑，是一种情景独特性人格特质。其测量技术包括观察法、自陈法等。语言焦虑与学习者文化、信念、人格、性别等诸多变量有关，与学习成就呈负相关，对口语表达有显著的消极影响。

关于语言焦虑的性质，不同理论解释不同。语言编码缺失假说认为，语言才能是语言学习的主要影响因素，语言焦虑是语言学习过程中的"副产品"（才能不足导致学习不良，并引发语言焦虑）。其他理论并不认为焦虑是学习中的"副产品"。情感过滤假说认为,焦虑会引起语言学习中的情感过滤,降低学习效率。群体动力理论认为,学习者可能产生促进或衰减性学习焦虑,前者能增加学习努力程度,后者会降低学习努力程度,甚至导致回避学习。认知观点认为,焦虑会占用认知资源,降低行为质量。

　　理论争议可能会长期存在,焦虑既可能是语言才能不足的结果,同时又会进一步损害学习行为。

Chapter 3 Teaching strategies for coping with language anxiety

Language classroom is the typical situation in which language anxiety may occur. That's why the most commonly used instrument for measuring language anxiety is the Foreign Language Classroom Anxiety Scale (FLCAS). Many items on the scale are related to the behaviors of the teacher. For example:

It frightens me when I don't understand what the teacher is saying in the foreign language.

I get upset when I don't understand what the teacher is correcting.

I am afraid that my language teacher is ready to correct every mistake I make.

Learning theories such as connectionism, constructivism, transformative learning, ACPO Model all suggest that the teacher can have a significant influence on the learners emotional reactions. This chapter focuses on some teaching strategies which are likely to help the teacher to manage students' anxiety in the language classroom.

3.1 Following the principles of connectionism

The learning theory of connectionism attaches great importance to rewarding. Connectionism interprets learning in terms of the interrelationships between stimulus, response and feedback. The early development of the connectionism (also called behaviorism) can be attributed to Pavlov, who investigated classical conditioning, and Skinner (as cited in Chen & Liu, 1997) who conducted research on operant conditioning. Classical conditioning is a kind of associative learning, which occurs when a neutral stimulus (conditioned stimulus) and a significant stimulus (unconditioned stimulus) are repeatedly paired. The result of this type of learning is that the organism/individual can gradually produce a behavioral response to the conditioned stimulus, which is called conditioned response. Operant conditioning develops via the feedback of reward or punishment following the behavior. In this type of learning, the frequency of a behavior may increase as a result of reward, and decrease as a result of punishment. Connectionism can explain some anxiety in both the first and the second language. In the first language, communication apprehension (CA) has been supposed to be a consequence of punishment relevant to the act of communication in the early years. When a child's attempts to speak the mother tongue are greeted with punishment from significant others, he/she will soon learn that the desirable behavior could be none other than keeping quiet. Consistent punishment may eventually create an apprehensive individual (Daly, 1991). In the second language, anxiety could be a result of the transference of the CA from the mother tongue, or a result of the unpleasant experience following or accompanying the behavior of learning or using the target language, among other sources/causes of anxiety. The language teacher him-/herself may be responsible for the development of the language anxiety experienced by some students due to the feedback given to the learners' language performance. It has been reported that frequent immediate correction of mistakes or errors (teacher feedback) is likely to increase the tension and apprehension of a second language learner (Hou, 2004).

To manage language anxiety, language teachers should provide general reward for learners' performance. Reward is a positive reinforcement when it is offered to the learners for their attempts to use the new language. Generous reward stresses that reward should not only be given for satisfactory performance, but also for imperfect performance. The teacher should also encourage peer learners to support and cheer each other even when the performances are unsatisfactory. Learning is a gradually improving process.

Negative feedbacks corresponding to imperfect performances of the learners, such as scolds, blames, or corrections of mistakes in the class, should not be frequently employed. Even when they are necessary, such feedbacks should not be regularly given immediately following the performances.

3.2　Following the principles of constructivism

Constructivism is a psychological theory which suggests that knowledge and meanings are generated by previous experience. The development of constructivism can be attributed to Piaget (as cited in Chen & Liu, 1997), who suggested that an individual internalizes knowledge via accommodation and assimilation. When the new experience is perceived as being consistent with the internal representations of the world, a person incorporates it into an existing framework (assimilation). When the new experience is perceived as being inconsistent with the internal representations, a person's internal representations of the external world are likely to be modified to fit the new experience (accommodation).

Constructivism regards learners as unique individuals with unique backgrounds, which help them to construct unique understandings of the same truth. According to constructivism, social interactions should be stressed, during which an individual can develop his/her thinking; the active roles of the learners, and the facilitating roles of instructors are emphasized, which are believed to foster learning; learning is considered to be more likely to occur if the new information is in proximity to, yet slightly above, the current level of development of the learner (Vygotsky, as cited in Chen & Liu, 1997). Constructivism encourages cooperative/collaborative learning. In the process of cooperation between peers, learners are supposed to be able to construct shared understanding of the same sets of truth.

In second language acquisition, cooperative learning has been suggested being capable of reducing language anxiety, increasing learner confidence, and stimulating motivation (Xing, 2007). Language teachers can foster cooperative learning by assigning group work or pair work in and outside the language classroom.

3.3　Following the principles of transformative learning

Transformative learning is an adult learning theory first advanced by

Mezirow (1975) who based his theory of transformative learning or learning for perspective transformation on the findings of a large study he conducted with mature women returning to college for further education. Transformative learning occurs when criticizing existing assumptions and meaning schemes brings about a significant reframing of an individual's meaning perspective (Mezirow, 1991). Meaning perspective has been defined by Mezirow as an individual's frame of reference through which meaning is constructed and all learning takes place. The frame of reference has two sub-components: habits of mind and points of view (Mezirow, 2000). It is through the process of transformational learning that people transform their taken-for-granted frames of reference so that they may generate beliefs and opinions that will prove more truthful or justified to guide actions.

Transformative learning theory explains how the belief system changes. Since dysfunctional beliefs (for example, perfectionism) are potential causes of language anxiety, language teachers should take advantage of the strategies of transformative learning, such as discussing, exposing and criticizing the learners dysfunctional beliefs, so as to bring about a transformation of those beliefs and consequently a reduction of their language anxiety.

3.4　Following the principles of ACPO Model

The ACPO Model stands for another set of learning principles, advanced by Brahmawong (2006). "A" stands for advance organizers, "C" stands for "concurrent organizers", and "P" stands for "post organizers". According to Brahmawong:

An advance organizer provides the learning plan to the students at the beginning of a lesson to let them know the topics, concepts or main ideas, objectives, learning activities, instruction media, learning resources, and evaluation process.

A concurrent organizer is a tool to help the students acquire the knowledge, read the require subject matter or know-how, get hand-on experiences, perform the assigned tasks, and check the results of their work.

A post organizer provides generalization or conclusion of what the students have learnt and how they should apply what they learn in different situations.

The ACPO Model conforms to constructivism. Organizers can help learners to waken or arouse their previous experience or background knowledge. By providing an expectation at the beginning of learning, an assisting tool while learning, and a direction on the generalization or conclusion following learning, organizers can make the language acquisition more structured, and less uncertain/ambiguous, which ultimately contributes to the reduction of language anxiety (Daly, 1991).

3.5 Other recommendations

(1) Developing learners' competence

Language anxiety is negatively related to language competence. Learners with a higher level of competence tend to have a lower level of anxiety. Developing the competence, therefore, can not only help learners approach the goal of learning, but also reduce their language anxiety. According to the relational model for managing foreign language anxiety proposed by Foss and Reitzel (1991), language teachers can (a) increase learners' communication competence by means of enhancing the motivation, (b) help learners grasp the behavioral patterns and strategies for communication in a given situation, (c) develop learners' skills for successful conversation in the new language, (d) raise learners' consciousness that an unsatisfactory outcome can still reflect competence if it is comparatively superior to its alternatives, and (e) help learners create a context that facilitates language learning (Spielberg and Cupach, 1984, cited in Foss and Reitzel, 1991).

(2) Raising learners' awareness of the phenomenon of anxiety

One way to raise awareness of the phenomenon of anxiety is anxiety graphing (Foss and Reitzel, 1991), which requires charting anxiety about a conversation immediately after it occurs so as to better understand the nature of one's anxiety, and to notice that learning the new language is not consistently anxiety provoking. Teachers can encourage students to write about their anxieties to a certain imaginary person, to write about their feelings and advices on language learning, and to share the writings with peer learners. Once students are aware that language anxiety is a common phenomenon among learners, they tend to support and encourage each other, which may alleviate their anxiety.

(3) Teaching learners a variety of strategies

Teachers should help learners grasp various strategies to deal with language anxiety, such as relaxation methods (e.g., enjoying light music or good humor), using positive self – talk (e.g., "I can do it", "I am a gifted learner", etc.), risk taking in learning, self – rewarding for satisfactory performance, establishing appropriate expectations (Oxford, 1990), and so on.

3.6 Summary in Chinese

语言课堂是语言焦虑发生的典型环境，为了降低语言焦虑，教师可采取如下策略。

第一，遵循联想主义有关原则。按照联想主义，学习是"刺激"—"反应"—"反馈"之间建立联系的过程。奖励或者惩罚性反馈会影响行为的频率。在第一语言中，交际恐惧被认为是早年交际行为受到惩罚的结果。在第二语言中，焦虑可能从第一语言交际恐惧迁移而来，也可能因语言学习或使用伴随的不愉快体验而产生。为了降低语言焦虑，教师应为学生的语言尝试多提供正强化或积极反馈，纠错要有选择性且讲究策略。

第二，遵循构建主义有关原则。按照构建主义，每个学习者均为独特的个体，各自拥有独特的经验背景。对于同一事实，学习者的独特背景会导致其产生独特的理解。构建主义强调合作学习。通过合作学习和同辈交流，学生有望对同样的事实构建一致的理解。二语教学中，合作学习可以降低语言焦虑，增强自信和动机。教师在课内外应当增加小组合作学习活动。

第三，借鉴转换学习有关策略。转换学习是一种成人学习理论，它强调通过批评既有认识，来重塑个人意义视角（思维习惯和观点），以产生更加正确合理的信念和看法来指导行为。转换学习强调的是信念体系的改变。适应不良的信念属于语言焦虑的潜在原因，教师应利用转换学习策略，诸如讨论、暴露、批评等来转变学生适应不良的信念。

第四，借鉴 ACPO 模型有关策略。ACPO 模型是一套教学原则。"A"代表"学前组织"，"C"代表"学中组织"，"P"代表"学后组织"。学前组织强调在课程开始前，向学生提供学习计划；学中组织强调在教学过程中，给学生提供支持和帮助；学后组织强调在教学之后，给学生提供学习内容的概括或总结。教师遵循 ACPO 模型可将语言教学活动组织得有条不紊，能够减少语言学习中的不确定性或模糊因素，从而降低学生的语言焦虑。

第五，注重学生的语言能力培养。培养能力不仅可以帮助学习者实现学习目标，还可以减轻他们的语言焦虑。根据语言焦虑控制模型，教师应帮助学生掌握在具体情境中的沟通模式和交流策略，增强他们的学习动机，纠正其认知误区，创造一个促进语言学习的良好环境。

第六，增强学生对语言焦虑的意识。教师可采用不同方法增强学生对焦虑的意识。一种典型方法是教会学生绘制焦虑曲线图。教师也可以鼓励学生向某个想象的朋友写信，倾诉自己的焦虑，并与同学分享这些内容。增强对彼此焦虑的意识，有助于控制或减轻自己的焦虑情绪。

Chapter 4　Relaxation techniques for coping with language anxiety

Relaxation techniques include, progressive muscle relaxation, diaphragm breathing, autogenic training (Benor 1996), guided imagery (Tusek, et al., 1997), mindfulness meditation (Kwee, 1995), biofeedback (Schwartz et al., 2017), hypnosis (Orne, 1959), and so on. Those techniques (emotion regulation strategies) are widely used to achieve physical and/or mental relaxation. Language anxiety is commonly accompanied by tension, which may not always be noticed by the person in anxiety. Relaxation techniques can reduce anxiety by counteracting the tension going with it.

4.1　Progressive muscle relaxation

4.1.1　Rationale of progressive muscle relaxation

In a threatening situation, animals may feel fearful or anxious, and the brain sends messages to the body to prepare for action, either running away or fighting (flight-or-fight response). To adapt to the need of the action, the muscle gets tensed. The muscle tension accompanying fear is therefore a reaction which has its evolutionary significance. Over time, this reaction has developed into a common response to fear. When it is not necessary for survival, this flight-or-fight reaction may result in a lot of uncomfortable symptoms like sweating or fast heart rate or shivering, which have a negative impact on our daily behavior and performance.

Anxiety, as we know, is a fear that is indirectly related to an object. The muscle tension accompanying anxiety is a common phenomenon familiar to all of us. Sometimes, the tension may be so weak that we are not aware of it; other times, it can be so strong that we can not behave normally. If the tense lasts for a long time, we may feel uncomfortable or painful.

Anxiety can be alleviated by means of reducing the accompanying tension. In one of his masterpieces, *What Is an Emotion?*, William James (1884) put forward a revolutionary idea of how the body affects the feelings:

If we fancy some strong emotion, and then try to abstract from our consciousness of it all the feelings of its bodily symptoms, we find we have nothing left behind.

In other words, James believed that nothing is left behind if we can remove all bodily symptoms from a strong emotion. Anxiety can be greatly reduced if we can abstract the muscle tension from it, or get into a state of complete physical relaxation. In fact, anxiety and physical relaxation are incompatible. One cannot be relaxed and feel anxious simultaneously.

Progressive muscle relaxation is a physical therapy created by American physician, Edmund Jacobson (1938), at the beginning of the 20th century (termed progressive relaxation at first). The purpose was to achieve mental repose by progressively getting rid of all muscular tensions. It was later developed and adapted by many other experts, but the essence of systematically tightening and releasing isolated muscle groups remains. How can tightening and releasing muscle groups bring about relaxation? Imagine, for instance, you have been carrying a load of 5 kilograms on your shoulder. You are most likely to feel an obvious tension in your muscle. The entire load is then removed from you all of a sudden. What will you feel in your muscle? It is an obvious relaxation. Suppose you have been carrying a load of 0.5 kilogram, what will you notice in your muscle when the load is suddenly removed from you? It is probably a small relaxation or no relaxation at all, because the load is not heavy enough to cause a great muscle tension when it is on you. Clearly, it is easier to make the muscle to relax from a state of higher level of tension than from a state of lower level of tension. In other words, relaxation is more likely to occur when the muscle has experienced a noticeable tension. The muscular tension related to anxiety is usually a moderate one which may be unnoticeable to people. In progressive muscle relaxation, the exaggerated tightening of the muscle is expected to bring about a noticeable feeling of relaxation. Once skillful at the exercise, you will be capable of identifying tension in any group of muscles and relaxing yourself wherever and whenever you want to. In a setting that is likely to cause language anxiety, you can quickly induce muscle relaxation, which further results in comfort and peacefulness, leaving no chance for the occurrence of language anxiety. To make it effective, you have to perform the procedure correctly and routinely.

4.1.2 Muscle groups and the methods for tensing them

There are many muscle groups in our body. To tense and relax them systematically in the procedure of progressive muscle relaxation, you have to remember not only the names of the muscle groups involved, but also the methods for tensing them. Table 4.1 provides a list of the primary muscle groups and the corresponding treatments.

Table 4.1　Primary muscle groups and the ways for tensing them

Muscle groups	Ways for tensing
Feet	Curl the toes downward.
Lower legs and calves	Point the toes upward.
Upper legs and thighs	Press the heels toward the floor if one is seated; straighten the legs if one is lying down.
Buttocks	Press them together.
Abdomen and chest	Breathe in deeply.
Hands and lower arms	Clench the hands into fists.
Upper arms	Raise the forearms toward the shoulders.
Shoulders	Raise them toward the ears, or pull them back/forward.
Neck	Bring the chin slowly toward the chest, or turn the head to the right/left.
Mouth, jaws, and cheeks	Smile broadly, or open the mouth widely, or purse the lips as if you are to whistle.
Lips	Purse them together.
Tongue	Press it against the roof/bottom of the mouth, or extend it, or retract it.
Eyes	Close/open them (contact lenses are to be removed if there are).

continued

Muscle groups	Ways for tensing
Forehead	Raise your eyebrows to wrinkle the forehead into a deep frown (contact lenses are to be removed if there are).

Some muscle groups have several alternative ways to be tensed and relaxed. When practicing progressive muscle relaxation, a person can choose one of them based on his preference.

4.1.3 Procedure for the practice of progressive muscle relaxation

(1) Selecting a place without distraction

As a beginner, you had better perform progressive muscle relaxation in a place with no distractions or disturbances. Turn off the TV, radio, or handset if there is. Use a soft or dim lighting if in a room. Play a relaxing music if it can help you relax. When you become skillful at the exercise, you can perform it anywhere in any condition.

(2) Loosening or removing things blocking the practice

Loosen your tight or uncomfortable clothes and shoes. Remove your contact lens, jewelry, watch, tie or collar if there are.

(3) Getting into the right posture

Sit at ease in a chair, or lie down on a bed. If you are sitting, keep your head and neck erect, you back naturally and comfortably upright. Keep your upper legs parallel with the ground and your lower legs upright. The distance between your knees should be approximately equal to the distance between the two ends of your shoulders. Close your eyes if that makes you feel comfortable. However, if you feel bothered with your eyes closed, you may simple keep them open.

(4) Tightening and relaxing the muscle groups

The technique requires a practitioner to relax the muscle groups via a two-step process. Firstly, focus on a muscle group, and tense (but not strain) it for a few seconds while breathing in, deliberately feeling the tension resulting from the tightening. Secondly, release the tension while breathing out, noticing the relaxation that follows. Every time when the tension is set free, the muscle will become more relaxed and comfortable than prior to the tensing. After a pause of a few seconds, go on with a new group of muscles. Following a certain sequence, all the muscle groups in the body are to be tensed and relaxed in turns.

4.1.4 Script for progressive muscle relaxation

This script for progressive muscle relaxation is a text which is designed to help you correctly practice the exercise. You can learn it by heart and follow it in you practice, have a friend direct you through it, or read it aloud and record your reading for your personal use.

Script

Take several deep, diaphragmatic breaths. Focus your attention on your breathing. Then proceed with the following steps:

Now pay attention to your left foot. Curl the toes downwards and tighten the muscle of your left foot as you breathe in, noticing the tension. Hold for about 5 seconds… and release the tension as you breathe out, feeling the relaxation that is left.

Pause for approximately 10 seconds and breathe normally, meditating on the difference between the tension and relaxation.

Now pay attention to your right foot. Curl the toes downwards and tighten the muscle of your right foot as you breathe in, noticing the tension. Hold for about 5 seconds … and release the tension as you breathe out, feeling the relaxation that is left.

Pause for approximately 10 seconds and breathe normally, meditating on the difference between the tension and relaxation.

Now flex your left foot as you breathe in, pointing the toes up towards your head, and noticing the tension in the left calf. Hold for about 5 seconds… and release the tension as you breathe out, feeling the relaxation that is left.

Pause for approximately 10 seconds and breathe normally, meditating on the difference between the tension and relaxation.

Now flex your right foot as you breathe in, pointing the toes up towards your head, and noticing the tension in the right calf. Hold for about 5 seconds… and release the tension as you breathe out, feeling the relaxation that is left.

Pause for approximately 10 seconds and breathe normally, meditating on the difference between the tension and relaxation.

Now press your left heel toward the floor to tense your left thigh as you inhale if you are seated, or tense your left thigh by straightening your left leg as you inhale if you are lying down, noticing the contraction in the left thigh. Hold for about 5 seconds⋯ and release the tightening as you exhale, feeling the relaxation that is left.

Pause for approximately 10 seconds and breathe normally, noticing the difference between the tension and relaxation.

Now press your right heel toward the floor to tense your right thigh as you inhale if you are seated, or tense your right thigh by straightening your right leg as you inhale if you are lying down, noticing the contraction in the right thigh. Hold for about 5 seconds⋯ and release the tightening as you exhale, feeling the relaxation that is left.

Pause for approximately 10 seconds and breathe normally, noticing the difference between the tension and relaxation.

Now press your buttocks together to tighten the muscles as you breathe in, noticing the tension in this area. Hold for about 5 seconds⋯ and release the tightening as you breathe out, feeling the relaxation that is left.

Pause for approximately 10 seconds and breathe normally, noticing the difference between the tension and relaxation.

Now breathe in deeply to tense the muscles within your abdomen, noticing the tension. Hold for about 5 seconds⋯ and release the tightening as you breathe out, feeling the relaxation that is left.

Pause for approximately 10 seconds and breathe normally, noticing the difference between the tension and relaxation.

Now tense the muscles of your left hand and lower arm by clenching your left hand into a fist as you inhale, noticing the tension. Hold for about 5 seconds⋯and release the tightening as you exhale, feeling the relaxation that is left.

Pause for approximately 10 seconds and breathe normally, noticing the difference between the tension and relaxation.

Now tense the muscles of your right hand and lower arm by clenching your right hand into a fist as you inhale, noticing the tension. Hold for about 5 seconds… and release the tightening as you exhale, feeling the relaxation that is left.

Pause for approximately 10 seconds and breathe normally, noticing the difference between the tension and relaxation.

Now raise your left forearm toward the shoulder to tense the muscles of your left upper arm as you breathe in, noticing the tension. Hold for about 5 seconds…and release the tightening as you breathe out, feeling the relaxation that is left.

Pause for approximately 10 seconds and breathe normally, thinking about the difference between the tension and relaxation.

Now raise your right forearm toward the shoulder to tense the muscles of your right upper arm as you breathe in, noticing the tension. Hold for about 5 seconds… and release the tightening as you breathe out, feeling the relaxation that is left.

Pause for approximately 10 seconds and breathe normally, thinking about the difference between the tension and relaxation.

Now raise both of your shoulders toward your ears to tense the muscles in this area as you inhale, noticing the tension in your shoulders. Hold for about 5 seconds… and release the tightening as you exhale, feeling the relaxation that is left.

Pause for approximately 10 seconds and breathe normally, thinking about the difference between the tension and relaxation.

Now bring your chin slowly toward your chest to tense the muscles in your neck as you inhale, noticing the tension in this area. Hold for about 5 seconds… and release the tightening as you exhale, feeling the relaxation that is left.

Pause for approximately 10 seconds and breathe normally, thinking about the difference between the tension and relaxation.

Now smile as broadly as you can to tense the muscles around your mouth, jaws and cheeks as you breathe in, noticing the tension in this area. Hold for about 5 seconds… and release the tightening as you breathe out, feeling the relaxation that is left.

Pause for approximately 10 seconds and breathe normally, meditating on the difference between the tension and relaxation.

Now purse your lips to tense the muscles here as you inhale, noticing the tension in this area. Hold for about 5 seconds⋯ and release the tightening as you exhale, feeling the relaxation that is left.

Pause for approximately 10 seconds and breathe normally, meditating on the difference between the tension and relaxation.

Now press your tongue against the roof of your mouth to tense the muscles here as you breathe in, noticing the tension in your tongue. Hold for about 5 seconds⋯ and release the tightening as you breathe out, feeling the relaxation that is left.

Pause for approximately 10 seconds and breathe normally, meditating on the difference between the tension and relaxation.

Now close your eyes to tense the muscles around your eyes as you inhale, noticing the tension in this area. Hold for about 5 seconds⋯ and release the tightening as you exhale, feeling the relaxation that is left.

Pause for approximately 10 seconds and breathe normally, meditating on the difference between the tension and relaxation.

Now raise your eyebrows to wrinkle the forehead into a deep frown to tense the muscles in this area as you breathe in, noticing the tension in this area. Hold for about 5 seconds⋯ and release the tightening as you breathe out, feeling the relaxation that is left.

Pause for approximately 10 seconds and breathe normally, meditating on the difference between the tension and relaxation.

Now focus your mind on your whole body, enjoying the warmth and comfort. Take a few deep breaths. Open your eyes slowly, stretch your arms and legs leisurely, and recover your normal behavior gently.

4.1.5 Tips for practicing progressive muscle relaxation

To make progressive muscle relaxation helpful, you have to use it with care. Here are some tips to be remembered.

(1) It is necessary to practice the technique under the guidance of an expert. If you have injuries, a history of injuries or other physical problems,

consult your doctors first. Never practice progressive muscle relaxation unless you get the permission and support of your doctors, because the muscle tensing may worsen the conditions.

(2) Perform the entire exercise once a day till you are capable of controlling your language anxiety. It requires a high level of persistence and a strong motivation to benefit from the exercise, as the effects can only be seen after prolonged practice (probably several weeks).

(3) Practice with an empty stomach so as to avoid negative influence on the digestion system. Never practice immediately after the use of alcohols or other intoxicants.

(4) Take care not to hurt yourself. Do not tighten a muscle group so hard as to cause hurt, pain or cramping. In fact, it's not necessary to tense the muscle really tightly. The strength is enough if it allows you to notice the tension. Nor should you tighten parts of your body which have caused you problems in the past. If you feel any pain or uncomfortable at a targeted muscle group, you can skip tensing it.

(5) When you tense a muscle, try not to disturb other muscles unless it is impossible. Imagination, such as visualizing the muscle group contracting while you are tensing it, or imagining a wave of warm liquid running over the muscle while releasing the tension, is beneficial for you to achieve the desired goal of tension and relaxation.

(6) The sequence of muscle groups to be treated is changeable. You can work from your feet to your head, or reverse the order and work from the head to the feet, or begin with your hands and arms.

Progressive muscle relaxation has been used in a variety of situations as a means of dealing with language anxiety. Quite a few modern studies have been done on the effect. The findings are promising. There are evidences suggesting a reduction of the levels of anxiety after routine performance of the technique. Practitioners tend to learn how to cope with language anxiety in stressful situations or settings. Moreover, long term practice can bring about a concentration of attention, an increase of self-confidence, a promotion of creativity, and an enhancement of general well-being.

4.2 Diaphragm breathing

Diaphragm breathing (belly breathing or abdominal breathing) is a relaxation exercise, in which breathing involves correct use of the diaphragm, a muscle separating the thoracic cavity and the abdominal cavity. It is also an important element in most other relaxation exercises. This technique can alleviate language anxiety by influencing the autonomous system.

The autonomous nerve system is composed of two parts, the sympathetic nervous system (fight – and – flight system) and the parasympathetic nervous system (rest – and – digest system). In the state of anxiety and tension, the sympathetic nervous system plays a dominant role. Our breath is shallow and irregular, the rate of heartbeat is fast, and the blood pressure is high. In other words, people are at a high level of emotional arousal. The high level of arousal may increase the feeling of anxiety and tension. In the state of peacefulness and comfort, the parasympathetic nervous system takes over the control. The breath is slow and regular, and the rate of heartbeat and blood pressure are both reduced to normal and healthy state. People are at a low level of emotional arousal in this state.

Diaphragm breathing can reduce anxiety by helping the parasympathetic nervous system to gain the upper hand in the autonomous system. Without the high level of emotional arousal, people tend to feel relaxed and calm.

Diaphragm breathing can force out the air buildup in the lungs, and enlarge the space for fresh air. We inhale through the nose and exhale through the mouth. When first practicing diaphragm breathing, you had better find a place without distraction. Sit in a chair or lie on a bed. Loosen tight clothing. Close your eyes. Calm and clear your mind. Focus on the regularity of your breathing.

As you inhale slowly and deeply through the nose, the belly expands (the diaphragm contracts and moves downward) while the chest is relatively immobile. Imagine that the air is breathed into the abdomen. As you exhale slowly and completely through your pursed mouth, the belly falls (the diaphragm relaxes and moves upward) while the chest is comparatively still. Imagine that the air is released from the abdomen. During the exercise, deliberately notice the movement of the belly. To feel the movement when you breathe, you can place one hand on the upper chest, and the other on the stomach (just below the rib cage). Repeat the breathing exercise during the whole session of practice.

Diaphragm breathing should be performed daily, with each session lasting for 5 to 15 minutes. Practice it under the guidance of an expert. Consult your doctor before trying the technique if you have health problems (e. g. , lung conditions like chronic obstructive pulmonary disease or asthma). Stop the exercise if you feel lightheaded or uncomfortable.

4.3 Autogenic training

Autogenic training (autogenic relaxation) is a progressive relaxation technique which is helpful for the relief of language anxiety, as well as some other problems (Ikonić & Hawes, 2017). It was created by German psychiatrist Johannes Heinrich Schultz (1932). Discovering that people experiencing hypnosis had the sensation of warmth and heaviness in the state of relaxation, Schultz developed this skill, hoping to induce hypnotic effect of relaxation through imagined warmth and heaviness. It is considered to be a self-hypnotic exercise, or a type of meditation.

Autogenic training is based primarily on self-talk or self-suggestion of warmth and heaviness in different parts (especially the limbs) of the body, which can bring about a feeling of peacefulness, relaxation and comfort. It is capable of regulating the autonomic nervous system, balancing the activity of the sympathetic and the parasympathetic nervous systems, reducing the rate of the heartbeat and breath, lowering the blood pressure, and benefiting the general health. Performing autogenic training routinely helps a person to control his mood and emotion, and enhance his self-concept and well-being.

To practice this exercise, you need to find a place without disturbances and distractions. Sit on a chair in a comfortable posture, or lie on a bed. Don't wear tight clothes. Close your eyes. Breathe slowly and deeply for 5 times to calm yourself and clear your mind. Now you can begin the series of quiet self-talk as you focus your attention on various parts of your body.

Focus on your left leg and foot. Tell yourself that the left leg and foot are pleasantly heavy for 5 times, noticing the pleasing heaviness.

Focus on your right leg and foot. Tell yourself that the right leg and foot are pleasantly heavy for 5 times, noticing the pleasing heaviness.

Focus on your left arm and hand. Tell yourself that the left arm and hand are pleasantly heavy for 5 times, noticing the pleasing heaviness.

Focus on your right arm and hand. Tell yourself that the right arm and hand are pleasantly heavy for 5 times, noticing the pleasing heaviness.

Focus on your left leg and foot. Tell yourself that the left leg and foot are comfortably warm for 5 times, noticing the comforting warmth.

Focus on your right leg and foot. Tell yourself that the right leg and foot are comfortably warm for 5 times, noticing the comforting warmth.

Focus on your left arm and hand. Tell yourself that the left arm and hand are comfortably warm for 5 times, noticing the comforting warmth.

Focus on your right arm and hand. Tell yourself that the right arm and hand are comfortably warm for 5 times, noticing the comforting warmth.

Focus on your heartbeat. Tell yourself that the heart beats stably, calmly and regularly for 5 times, noticing the stability, calmness and regularity of the heartbeat.

Focus on your breathing. Tell yourself that you breathe peacefully, calmly and regularly for 5 times, noticing the peacefulness, calmness and regularity of the breathing.

Focus on your abdomen. Tell yourself that the abdomen is comfortably warm for 5 times, noticing the comforting warmth.

Focus on your forehead. Tell yourself that the forehead is pleasantly cool for 5 times, noticing the pleasant coolness.

Focus on your whole body, and enjoy the wonderful sensation of heaviness, warmth, and relaxation.

Take a few slow and deep breaths, open your eyes slowly, and terminate the exercise.

After the autogenic training, you will feel tranquil, refreshed and relaxed. When you are skillful at the technique, you can induce relaxation quickly by noticing the warmth and heaviness in your body, whenever and wherever you experience or are likely to experience language anxiety. The self-talk can be replaced by the guidance of a therapist or an audio recording. To achieve a satisfactory effect, you had better perform it daily. This exercise does not suit children under 5 years old. Practice it under the guidance of a professional. Individual having heart problems, severe emotional or mental disorders, or other health problems must consult the doctor before practicing autogenic training. Give up the practice and consult the doctor if you experience any discomfort when practicing it.

4.4 Guided imagery

Guided imagery is a technique to be used to elicit relaxation through mental images. Different from other anxiety control techniques, guided imagery is dependent on a practitioner's use of all his senses. As an anxiety reduction exercise, it is very popular due to its effectiveness (Veena & Alvi, 2016; Nurhuda et al., 2019; Panneerselvam & Govindharaj, 2016; Dahbi, 2015). Guided imagery can quickly bring about a deep mental peace and physical relaxation, and help a person to get into a most favorable state for coping with language anxiety. Similar to daydreaming, it is easy to learn, and pleasant and convenient to practice. You can follow the guidance of a therapist or an audio recording, or simply use your imagination or memory to direct you.

As a beginning practitioner, you have to select a quiet place where you will not be disturbed or distracted. Loosen your tight clothing. Remove your collar, tie or other uncomfortable things. Turn off the handset and the TV. Sit on a seat in a comfortable posture, or lie down on a bed. Do not cross your legs. Close your eyes, and keep a smiling facial expression. Breathe slowly and deeply for 5 times to quiet yourself and concentrate your mind. Talk to yourself quietly that you are breathing in peacefulness, calmness, comfort and enjoyment. Visualize that your worry, nervousness, bothering thoughts, and tension are blown into the distant space as you exhale. Imagine a sense of relaxation moving slowly and comfortably from your head to your feet. Feel that you are totally calm, serene, satisfied and at ease. Dream of or recall a scene or location in which you can feel most free, relaxed, comfortable, safe and peaceful (e. g., a beach, mountain, field, garden, forest, or park). Give a vivid and fascinating depiction of the scene or location with positive adjectives describing sight, sound, smell, color, taste, and/or touch, so as to stimulate your senses. The more sensory attributes involved, the better the effect. Guided imagery is dependent on the lively use of various sensations. For example, you can imagine:

I am lying reclined on the soft green grass, enjoying the pleasant warm spring sunshine. The sky is as blue as the ocean. A few white clouds are moving slowly in it. There are some beautiful swans flying high up in the air. Standing around me are a few green trees, whose leaves are swaying leisurely in the gentle breeze. I can hear the pleasant chirps of happy birds in the tree. There are some tiny flowers in the grass, which are giving forth refreshing sweet smell. No one else is nearby. All the beautiful sight is for me to enjoy alone.

The more items and details you can imagine, the more effective the technique tends to be. You can completely immerse yourself in the scene and appreciate the environment for as long as possible, trying to avoid thinking of the troubles of your daily life. When you return to reality, deliberately feel the sense of relaxation, peacefulness and comfort. Guided imagery can also focus on cheerful incidents, such as being praised by the English teacher, getting a high score on a language test, winning a top honor in a game, meeting your beloved person, participating in an enjoyable party, having a delicious dinner in a long-dreamed 5-star hotel, going on a journey to a country on the other side of the globe, getting a patent for your invention, and so on. This technique is frequently practiced with other relaxation exercises. Guided imagery can not only help people reduce tension and language anxiety, but also provide many other health benefits. When you are familiar with it, you can perform the exercise in any place at any time.

4.5 Mindfulness meditation

Mindfulness is derived from traditional Buddhist practice. Being mindful means being aware of the present moment experience (Qureshi, 2016). Mindfulness meditation does not mean clearing one's mind. Instead, one learns to observe, nonjudgmentally and compassionately, his present moment thoughts, feelings and behaviors from the perspective of an outsider or onlooker. Mindfulness meditation can not only bring about relaxation, but also produce many other benefits. Performing the exercise routinely can gradually increase an individual's consciousness of the ongoing thoughts, feelings and behaviors, promote the meta–cognition and psychological well being, and reduce language anxiety, test anxiety, general anxiety, and other emotional problems (Van De Weijer-Bergsma et al., 2014; Schonert–Reichl et al., 2015; Raes et al., 2014; López-González et al., 2016). Nowadays, Mindfulness is widely practiced or studied in education settings (Albrecht, 2016; Felver & Jenning, 2016; Felver et al., 2016; Bluth et al., 2016; Galante et al., 2018).

A popular mindfulness meditation technique is called body scan, which involves sweeping through various regions of the body with one's attention, and intentionally feeling the sensations in each part at the moment.

During the body scan one observes what's going on mentally and physically, and accepts all the sensations without reactions, judgments, or intention to change anything. If the mind wanders, one just needs to bring it back.

Practicing body scan regularly can enhance awareness of the mind–body relationship. Mind and body have mutual influence. If the mind is anxious, the body is tense. The tension of the body can further magnify the anxiety of the mind. Being aware of the reciprocal impacts, one can reduce the negative influence which results from the interaction between the mind and the body by refraining the mind from reacting to the body sensation.

The time needed for one session of body scan ranges from a few minutes to half an hour or longer. If you are too busy, you may prefer a brief body scan, in which a large area of the body (e.g., the legs) is treated as a whole. If you have enough time, you can perform a prolonged body scan, in which each small region of the body (e. g. , each toe) is scanned separately. In a detailed body scan, your can follow this route:

(1) Left leg: toes, sole, heel, sides of the foot, top of the foot, ankle, shin, calf, knee, kneecap, thigh, left hip;

(2) Right leg: toes, sole, heel, sides of the foot, top of the foot, ankle, shin, calf, knee, kneecap, thigh, left hip;

(3) Pelvis (pelvic bowl), buttocks, lower back, upper back, abdomen, chest, ribs, breasts, heart, lungs, shoulders, collarbones;

(4) Left arm: fingers, palm, back of hand, wrist, forearm, elbow, upper arm;

(5) Right arm: fingers, palm, back of hand, wrist, forearm, elbow, upper arm;

(6) Scalp (top, sides, back), face (ears, eyes, nose, mouth, jaws), tongue, throat.

You can use the words in the box here to examine your momentary feelings in a specific part of the body.

| warmth, coolness, dryness, wetness, tightness, tension, stiffness, numbness, softness, relaxation, pleasure, pain, discomfort, comfort, weightlessness, heaviness, expansion, contraction, tingling, itching, pulsing, pounding, throbbing, trembling, shivering, shaking, vibrating, sinking, etc. |

Before you begin, select a warm and secure place in which you are free from disturbance and distraction. Loosen your tight clothes. Remove your watch and tie. Turn off your handset. Sit, stand or lie in a comfortable position. Close your eyes. Take a few deep and slow breaths to calm your mind. Then you can begin the body scan following the guidance of a therapist, a professional, a friend, a recording, or your memory:

Curiously and nonjudgmentally examine your emotion (happiness, anger, anxiety, frustration, neutral emotion⋯)

Curiously and nonjudgmentally examine your breath system (What/where is attracting you attention? Notice the rising and falling of your abdomen as you breathe).

Now focus on the toes of the left foot. Curiously and nonjudgmentally examine the sensation of each toe in turn (How does each toe feel? Is it warm/cool/hot/cold? Is it dry/moist? Is it tense/relaxed? Is it itchy/painful? Is it in touch with the sock? Is there any feeling of pressure/heaviness/weightlessness/tingling? ...). Whether the sensation is pleasant or unpleasant, just accept it without the intention to change anything. When you become aware of a sensation, notice whether it is changing, and how it is changing. See whether you mind is inclined to produce any emotion (e.g., anxiety, anger, or happiness) to a sensation as you become aware of it. Just be conscious of and accept whatever occurs.

In similar ways, go on to scan other parts of your body.

When you finish scanning different parts, focus on the whole body, and examine the overall sensation. Then, you can terminate the exercise with a deep breath, open your eyes and return to reality.

4.6 Other relaxation related techniques

(1) Biofeedback

Biofeedback is a mind-body technique with which one gains awareness of the functions of one's physiological systems with the help of instruments or devices that display information on the activity of those systems, such as brainwaves, skin conductance, heart rate, breath rate, and so on. In biofeedback, a person is connected to electrical devices that detect and display relevant information about the activity or function of the body that are normally at the level of unconsciousness. With such information, one can learn to manipulate one's physiological functions to a certain degree. Biofeedback is effective for many emotional issues (Kassel, 2015).

Language anxiety is an emotional reaction, which is related to a series of physiological activities. With the help of biofeedback, one can alleviate his anxiety by intentionally changing the activities. As one becomes skillful, he can ultimately manipulate his physiological activities without the use of any devices.

For example, an electrodermograph (EDG) can be used to detect skin electrical activity related to anxiety (worry can raise the level of sweat and increase skin conductance). With the feedback, one can consciously reduce the skin conductance, which can lead to an alleviation of anxiety.

A photoplethysmograph can measure heart rate and heart rate variability (HRV), which can be used by a person to stabilize his heart beat and reduce the level of tension.

Biofeedback can be used with deep breathing, progressive muscle relaxation, guided imagery, autogenic training and mindfulness meditation to increase the effectiveness (help the practitioner to better control the blood pressure, heat rate, and muscle tension, which leads to deeper relaxation).

2) Hypnosis

Hypnosis is a state of consciousness which involves concentrated attention, decreased peripheral awareness, and an improved tendency to follow guidance. When used as therapy for treatment of behavioral, psychological, or physical problems, hypnosis is call hypnotherapy. Hypnotherapy has been found to be capable of increasing one's ability to concentrate his attention, and regulate his emotion, including language anxiety (Valentine et al., 2019).

In a hypnosis state, one experiences a phase which helps him release the tension, focus the mind, and become more likely to react to guidance from a therapist or oneself.

In a state of hypnosis, a person is inclined to think, feel, or perceive in consistence with the guidance regardless whether the guidance is in agreement with one's perception of the actual item in reality. The experience in hypnosis may change an individual's memory or pattern of thinking, which may have an effect on one's cognition and behavior in real life.

Let's suppose you are afraid of presentation performance in the front of the classroom. In a hypnosis state, under the guidance of a therapist or yourself, you can visualize a past anxiety-provoking event of presentation as if it had been an enjoyable experience, and then imagine a future event of presentation which delights you. In a deep state of relaxation, such visualization or imagination is unlikely to induce fear or symptoms of fear.

4.7　Summary in Chinese

　　语言焦虑一般伴随有紧张反应，消除了紧张便可以缓解焦虑。消除紧张的常用放松技术有如下几种（如有健康问题，需咨询医生，获得同意后方可练习）。

　　第一，渐进肌肉放松。该技术要求依次对各个肌肉群进行系统的收紧和松弛，涉及的部位有脚、小腿、大腿、臀部、腹部、胸部、手部、前臂、上臂、肩膀、颈部、口腔、眼睛、额头等。熟练后可同时对多个肌肉群放松。练习渐进肌肉放松前当去掉妨碍放松的佩戴品，如隐形眼镜等。收紧时不要用力过度，以免伤害自己。

　　第二，腹式呼吸（深度呼吸）。练习时可将两手分别置于腹部和胸部，随慢慢呼吸，感受腹部起伏而胸部平稳。

　　第三，自生训练。这也是一种渐进式放松技术，它主要基于针对身体不同部位（尤其是四肢），自我默念或暗示的温暖和沉重，来产生宁静、放松和舒适的感觉。熟练掌握后，个人可随时通过注意身体的温暖和沉重来快速放松。

　　第四，意象引导。这是一种意象引发平静和放松的技术。练习者需闭上眼睛，想象或回忆一个场所，在此自己可以感受最大程度的自由、放松、安全和宁静。然后使用描述视觉、声音、气味、颜色或触觉的积极形容词，对场景进行生动而迷人的想象描绘，以刺激自己的感官。涉及的感觉属性和细节越多，效果越好。

　　第五，正念冥想。它是指意识对当前身心状态的专注。在冥想中，个人超越自我，从旁观者的角度，带着同情、接纳和好奇的心态，用意识的"聚光灯"观照自己当前的状态。冥想方法很多，常用的一种是身体扫描，即通过依次对身体不同部位状态的内观达到放松目的。

　　第六，其他方法。其他放松方法有生物反馈、催眠等。生物反馈是个人借助仪器显示生理状态信息，达到自我控制生理功能的方法。通过反馈信息，个人可以有效进行自我放松。催眠是指通过催眠师或自我诱导，进入一种特殊意识状态。在这种状态下，个人对周围事物的知觉降低，注意力高度集中，容易接受催眠师或自己的提示。催眠不仅能带来高度放松，也能通过想象改变对焦虑刺激的反应模式。

Chapter 5 Systematic desensitization and cognitive behavioral therapies for language anxiety

This chapter introduces two types of psychotherapies applicable to language anxiety, systematic desensitization and cognitive-behavioral therapies (CBT). They belong to the first and the second generation of behavior therapies respectively. The first generation emphasizes modification of behaviors; the second generation stresses change of dysfunctional thoughts or both thoughts and behaviors. Like relaxation techniques, systematic desensitization and cognitive-behavioral therapies are widely used emotion regulation strategies (Zhang, 2017; Brown et al., 2019).

5.1 Systematic desensitization

5.1.1 The rationale of systematic desensitization

When people experience an anxiety, they have a tendency to evade the feared scenario, setting, situation, event or item (stimulus). This evasion can temporarily alleviate anxiety. The alleviation, in turn, may reinforce the tendency of evading the feared stimulus. This is called operant conditioning. The objective of systematic desensitization (also known as graduated exposure therapy) is to help individuals overcome avoidance by gradually exposing them to the feared stimulus, until it no longer evokes any anxiety. This technique was developed by a South African psychiatrist Wolpe (1958). In one experiment in Wits University, cats were given electric shock while eating so as to condition them to refuse to eat in a confined space. By feeding them first in remotely similar situations, and later in more and more similar situations, Wolf discovered that the cats was able to gradually overcome their conditioned fear and anxiety. Inspired by his observation, Wolpe created systematic desensitization. As a type of behavioral modification strategy, this technique conforms to the principle of classical conditioning and the idea that what has been learnt can be unlearnt.

5.1.2 Procedure of systematic desensitization

Most anxiety-provoking ← → Least anxiety-provoking	Lecturing at the English speech contest.
	↑
	Lecturing at the English speech contest rehearsal.
	↑
	Practicing with a few friends for the English speech contest.
	↑
	Practicing with parents for the English speech contest.
	↑
	Practicing alone for the English speech contest.
	↑
	Watching friends lecturing at the English speech contest.
	↑
	Registering for the English speech contest.
	↑
	Being persuaded to participate in the English speech contest.
	↑
	Hearing the news of the English speech contest.

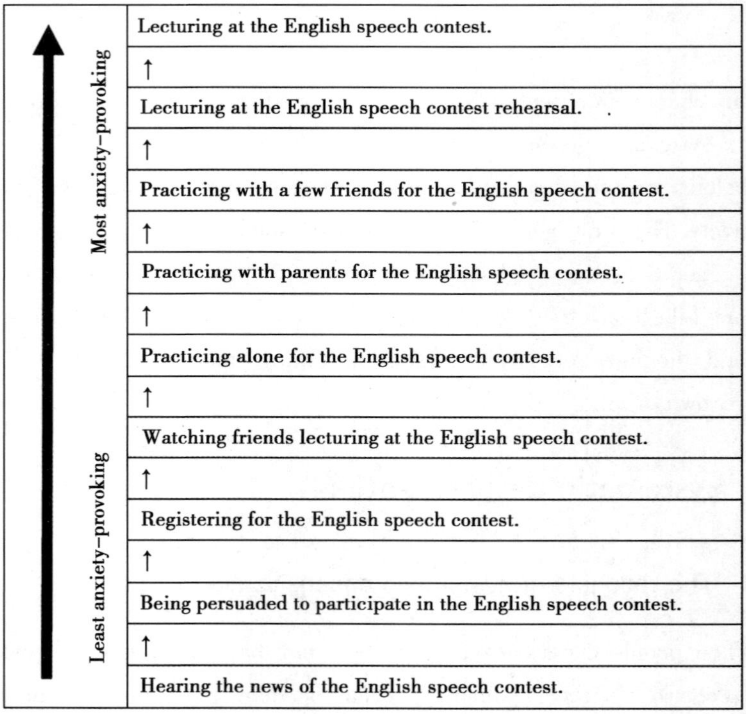

Figure 5.1 An example of speaking anxiety hierarchy

Three stages are involved in the therapy of systematic desensitization. Firstly, the practitioner has to establish an anxiety-provoking stimulus hierarchy (anxiety hierarchy), which is a most important part of the procedure. He has to list all the stimuli which are likely to evoke the same category of anxiety problems. Every stimulus is provided a ranking based on the severity of anxiety it is likely to evoke. Those anxiety stimuli are arranged in a hierarchy, beginning with the least anxiety-arousing to the greatest anxiety-arousing. If an individual is suffering from different categories of anxiety problems, the stimuli in each category are to be ranked and coped with separately. Figure 5.1 and Figure 5.2 demonstrate two examples of anxiety hierarchies.

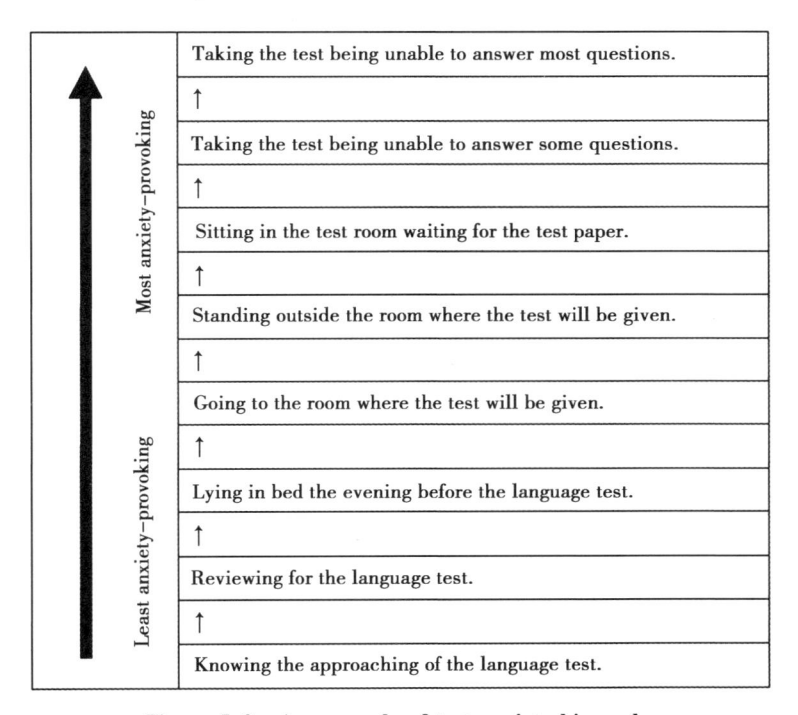

Most anxiety-provoking ↑	Taking the test being unable to answer most questions.
	↑
	Taking the test being unable to answer some questions.
	↑
	Sitting in the test room waiting for the test paper.
	↑
	Standing outside the room where the test will be given.
	↑
	Going to the room where the test will be given.
	↑
	Lying in bed the evening before the language test.
	↑
	Reviewing for the language test.
	↑
Least anxiety-provoking	Knowing the approaching of the language test.

Figure 5.2 An example of test anxiety hierarchy

Secondly, the practitioner needs to learn relaxation exercises, such as progressive muscle relaxation, guided imagery, autogenic training, or diaphragmatic breathing, which he has to employ in the third stage. Relaxation is the weapon to counteract anxiety.

Thirdly, an association of relaxation with the anxiety-provoking item has to be created. Relaxation and anxiety can not coexist due to the mutual inhibition between them. When a stimulus is associated with relaxation, it will no longer be linked to anxiety. To develop the desired pairing, the practitioner has to get into a state of relaxation and comfort through the relaxation exercise, and imagine or confront the least anxiety-provoking item in the anxiety hierarchy. If feeling anxious, he has to give up the attempt and comfort himself through the relaxation exercise, and try to deal with the item next time. When feeling no anxiety toward the stimulus, he can move on to imagine or confront the next item in the hierarchy which is more anxiety-provoking. In this way, the practitioner will ultimately become insensitive (desensitized) to all the items, including the most anxiety – provoking ones in the hierarchy. If having much trouble with an item, the practitioner has to divide it up further, and keep trying the items repeatedly. The gradual exposure will eventually help one become desensitized.

Systematic desensitization can be self-administered, or administered by a trained professional. It is a slow process. The number of sessions needed is dependent on the severity of the anxiety. Generally 6 – 8 sessions are required, though it has been found that more sessions tend to result in better effect. The practice is over when the expected goal is achieved.

5.1.3 Effects of and tips for systematic desensitization

Systematic desensitization has been used or studied in various settings to help people overcome anxiety since its publication (Sharma, 2018; Aihie & Igbineweka, 2018; Otta & Ogazie, 2014; Ifeanyi et al., 2015; Rajiah et al., 2014). It is quite effective for learned anxiety (McGrath et al., 1990). Language anxiety is certainly a learned anxiety, because it is an emotional response originating from the course of language learning.

The exposure can be accomplished in different ways. Two of the most frequently used are exposure in imagination and exposure in reality. Exposure in imagination means that the practitioner is exposed to the anxiety stimulus through imagination, while exposure in reality means that the practitioner is exposed to the anxiety stimulus in a real situation. Needless to say, exposure in reality is more effective than exposure in imagination. When one is confronting an imagined stimulus, he is aware that what he faces is not real. Moreover, people may differ in the aptitude for imagination. If one is incapable of producing a vivid anxiety stimulus, the exposure can not have a strong impact on him. Even though exposure in imagination poses drawbacks, it is more widely employed due to its convenience.

In the era of information technology, computer simulated exposure (virtual reality) can be used in place of exposure in reality. If the quality of simulation is satisfactory, simulated exposure can produce similar effect as exposure in reality for some anxiety stimuli.

In fact, with sufficient exposure to the threatening items, one can become desensitized even without the relaxation or hierarchical procedure. For example, many people having the experience of language test anxiety can become desensitized by taking language tests repeatedly.

It is also plausible to add an element of cognitive modification to the exercise of systematic desensitization. For example, you can imagine a threatening situation (anxiety stimulus), and then replace the outcome which was responsible for your previous anxiety with an agreeable outcome. You may be afraid of being negatively evaluated by your friends for your presentation. When you are practicing systematic desensitization, you may as well imagine that your presentation is highly appreciated by your friends as well as your language teacher.

To motivate yourself to stick to the practice of systematic desensitization, you can list a few reasons for your performance (e.g., the top 5 reasons for your choice to overcome your language anxiety). When creating an anxiety hierarchy, you can first identify the most anxiety-provoking stimulus, and then the least one. After the identification of the extremes, it is time to add the in-between stimuli. Including as many in-between items as possible will foster the effect. A practicable plan or schedule for your practice should be worked out and followed without interruption.

5.2 Cognitive behavioral therapies

CBTs are psychotherapies that aim at coping with anxiety and other mental problems by modifying dysfunctional thoughts, beliefs, or patterns of thinking (cognitions) and behaviors. They combine the fundamental principles of cognitive and behavioral therapies.

5.2.1 History of CBTs

Two of the earliest and most influential types of CBTs are rational emotive behavior therapy (REBT) and cognitive therapy (CT).

REBT was created by Albert Ellis in the mid-1950s (Dryden, 2001), and developed by Ellis himself as well as many other experts in the following decades. REBT emphasizes the role of beliefs in psychological problems. When advancing the theory, Ellis was influenced by the view of the Stoic philosopher Epictetus who claimed that people are not disturbed by things, but by the views they take of them (Ellis, 2004). Ellis further developed this philosophic view into his A-B-C theory of personality. "A" is an adversity or activating event, "B" is the belief about "A", and "C" is the emotional or behavioral consequence. The theory proposes that the effect of "A" on "C" is decided by the mediate factor "B". In other words, it is the "B" that is directly related to the "C". Faced with the same event ("A"), different beliefs ("B") may result in different emotional and behavioral consequences ("C"). Based on the rationale of the A-B-C theory of personality, REBT attributes emotional problems such as anger, anxiety, and depression to irrational beliefs (rigid and extreme ideas), and considers the substitution of rational beliefs (flexible and non-extreme ideas) for the irrational ones as the remedy for the problems (Dryden, 2001). There are four sets of irrational beliefs, and four sets of corresponding rational substitutes. Table 5.5 demonstrates each set of beliefs with an example.

Table 5.1   Irrational and rational beliefs (Dryden, 2001)

Irrational Beliefs	Rational Beliefs
Demands "I must do well."	Full preferences "I want to do well, but I don't have to do so."
Awfulizing beliefs "I must do well, *and it's terrible if I don't.*"	Anti-awfulizing beliefs "I want to do well, but I don't have to do so. *It's bad if I don't do well but not terrible.*"
Low frustration tolerance beliefs "I must do well and *I can't bear it if I don't.*"	High frustration tolerance beliefs "I want to do well, but I don't have to do so. *When I don't do well, it's difficult to bear, but I can bear it.*"
Depreciation beliefs "I must do well and *I am a failure if I don't.*"	Acceptance beliefs "I want to do well, but I don't have to do so. *When I don't do well, I am not a failure, but only a fallible human being who fails to do well on this occasion.*"

To foster the substitution of beliefs, REBT requires the therapist to analyze the clients' beliefs, and help them to identify the irrational ideas, to dispute them, and finally to replace them with their rational counterparts (Weinrach, 1995). The final goal of REBT is not only to help clients overcome their present emotional problems, but also to change their philosophy and personality, which renders them to stay better and less disturbable in the future (Ellis, 1997).

CT was developed by Aaron T. Beck, an American psychiatrist (1964, 1967). Beck suggests that cognitive distortion contribute to negative view of oneself, the world, and future, and lead to emotional and behavioral problems. CT focuses on an individual's beliefs, such as his judgment, assessment, expectation, interpretation of events, and so on. It encourages one to consider his cognitive reactions to things as opinions or assumptions rather than as facts or hard truths, so that a person can objectively and carefully examine them, and arrive at new healthy views, which may further lead to beneficial or functional emotional and behavioral consequences. Once he has understood the rationale, a person can transfer the skills he learnt from CT to his daily life in the future to deal with various emotional problems.

CT highlights several cognitive distortions. An individual is required to memorize them, so that he can be on guard against arriving at problematic inferences. Those errors include all – or – nothing thinking, discounting the positive, overgeneralization, jumping to conclusions, mind reading, fortune telling, magnifying/minimizing, "should" statements, labeling, inappropriate blaming, and so on (Dobson, 2010).

Although REBT and CT are both independent theories, many people choose to combine them with other theories, and continually develop new types of CBTs to increase the therapeutic effect. The following sections focus on the introduction of mainstream CPT.

5.2.2 The rational of mainstream CPT

Different from traditional psychoanalysis, which focuses on the impact of early experience, mainstream CBT concentrates on solutions to problems in the present. It is based on the interrelationships between events, cognitions/

cognitive appraisal/thoughts, emotions and behaviors, as can be displayed with a simplified model by Wright, Basco & Thase (see Figure 5.3, as cited in Wright, 2006).

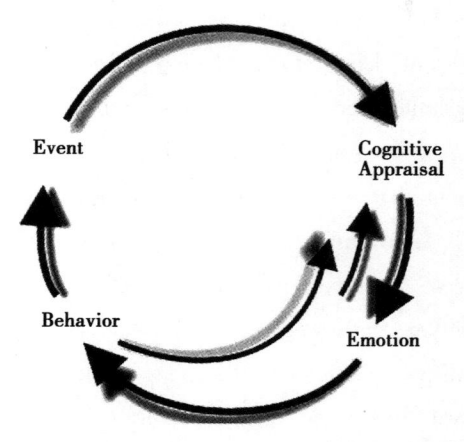

Figure 5.3 Basic cognitive behavior model
(Wright, 2006, p. 174)

Take a language test as an example. Failing the test is an activating event. Different students many have different thoughts (cognitive appraisals) on it. If a student thinks that the failure is an evidence of his poor language aptitude, he may have the emotion of anxiety. The anxiety may cause the behavior of avoiding language learning or practice, which is likely to lead to future failure. In other words, the student is trapped in a vicious cycle. Confronting the same failure, another student may interpret it as an evidence of lack of hard work. Such an interpretation is unlikely to produce anxiety. This student will most probably devote more effort to his study, which can prevent or reduce the probability of future failure. The second student is thus engaged in a healthy cycle. CBT can help individuals with maladaptive thoughts and behaviors understand the root of their problems, and overcome those problems through necessary changes.

5.2.3 Understanding cognitive distortions

Cognitive distortions are incorrect thoughts or patterns of thinking that are responsible for dysfunctional emotions or behaviors. Using CPT to cope with language anxiety, one has to understand not only the concept of language anxiety and its negative influence on learning, but also the cognitive distortions responsible for his language anxiety. Here are some major types of cognitive distortions.

(1) Mental filtering

Mental filtering refers to the way of thinking which concentrates on the unpleasant factors, neglecting all of the pleasant ones. Like seeing things through a pair of colored glasses, a person with mental filtering perceives only part of the reality. For example, after a presentation, a student focuses only on his poor pronunciation and feels bad about his performance, being oblivious of that fact that friends have been deeply impressed by his creative ideas.

(2) All-or-nothing thinking

All-or-nothing thinking is a way of thinking that considers only the extremes, without seeing any gradual changes in between. For instance, students who believe their pronunciation is either perfect or worst are showing all-or-nothing thinking.

(3) Overgeneralization

Overgeneralization refers to the thought or way of thinking which inappropriately generalizes the finding or experience one has on one occasion to many dissimilar occasions. One of your high school teachers, for example, ever pointed out your grammar mistakes in your speech, and you have since become so sensitive to grammar as to be afraid of speaking the language even if you are now studying in a university. You are displaying overgeneralization because your high school experience is unsuitably generalized to the university which is certainly quite different.

(4) Jumping to conclusions

Jumping to conclusions means arriving at conclusions without having enough information or evidence to guarantee the correctness of the conclusions. An example is, "My language aptitude must be very low, because I have failed the English test". This conclusion is vulnerable. There were numerous factors which might be responsible for failing the test.

(5) Catastrophizing

Catastrophizing is a way of thinking which magnifies the expected negative consequence of a slight incident to such a degree as to become a catastrophe. For example, you are catastrophizing if you are worried by the thinking that the misspelling of a word in your writing will ruin the whole paper.

(6) Rigid demanding

Rigid demanding refers to the way of thinking in which one rigidly demands oneself or others to behave in a specific way. Expressed in a sentence, rigid demanding usually contains "should", "must", "have to", "ought to", and so forth. For example, "One should not speak a foreign language before he can speak it correctly".

(7) Emotional reasoning

Emotional reasoning is a type of illogical reasoning which is based on one's feeling. For example, "I'm sure my language teacher dislikes me because I can feel it".

Listed above are the frequently seen cognitive distortions related to language anxiety. To reinforce your understanding, Table 5.2 presents an exercise. You are expected to match the thoughts in the left column with the cognitive distortion labels in the right.

Table 5.2   An exercise for recognizing cognitive distortions

Thoughts	Cognitive distortions
1) One should not make mistakes when he uses a foreign language.	a. Mental filtering
2) In spite of the fact that Zhang's English is better than most of his friends, he strongly believes his own feeling that he has no talent in language learning.	b. All-or-nothing thinking
3) I failed the CET 4 last year. There is no point in taking the test in the future.	c. Overgeneralization
4) Though praised by the teacher, Li Ping still felt bad about her writing because there were several mistakes in grammar.	d. Jumping to conclusions
5) He thought that it would be the end of the world if he couldn't get a score of 7.0 on the IELTS test.	e. Catastrophizing
6) He didn't reply to my English letter immediately. He must have thought poorly of the writing.	f. Rigid demanding
7) I will be a complete failure if I won't be able to answer all the questions correctly.	g. Emotional reasoning

Key: 1) →f; 2) →g; 3) →c; 4) →a; 5) →e; 6) →d; 7) →b.

5.2.4 Identifying cognitive distortions in thoughts

(1) Learning the difference between opinions and facts

Prior to discussing the identification of cognitive distortions, it is necessary to learn the difference between opinions and facts. A fact is a hard truth, while an opinion is a personal judgment. A fact is indisputable, while an opinion is arguable. Most people value and trust their personal opinions to such a degree as if they were incontrovertible facts, forgetting that opinions are something challengeable. Table 5.3 provides an exercise. You are expected to decide whether each statement in the left column is an opinion or a fact.

Table 5.3　　An exercise for distinguishing opinions from facts

1) The book is written in English.	Opinion ☐	Fact ☐
2) Language learning is as interesting as math.	Opinion ☐	Fact ☐
3) I failed the CET 4 last year.	Opinion ☐	Fact ☐
4) The CET 4 is difficult.	Opinion ☐	Fact ☐
Key: 1) fact; 2) opinion; 3) fact; 4) opinion		

It is easy. The first and third statements are facts, while the second and the fourth are opinions. Learning to distinguish between opinions and facts can help an individual realize that his thoughts are not always objective truths, and that they are subject to dispute and modification.

(2) Increasing awareness of thoughts provoking language anxiety

Language learners are prone to anxiety in situations where language is learned or used. What on earth are the thoughts relevant to anxiety? To catch those thoughts, one can visualize a situation or be in a real situation, imagine an event which makes him experience language anxiety, and deliberately focus on his mind to "see" what thought is responsible for the anxiety. Jotting down the event, thought, and consequences in the form of a journal, he will be able to analyze it for the distortions. For example, a language student can produce the following journal:

"In the English class this morning, Mr. Wang asked me to read the text which we had learnt. My reading was not fluent. I felt extremely anxious the whole class after the reading because I was sure that I had left a terrible impression on the teacher. My heart beat fast. I could not focus my attention on the lecture."

To clarify the information, we can separate the content into activating event, thought, emotion, and behavior/physical response, and put those elements in a worksheet (Table 5.4). It is better to give a rating of the levels of the emotional and/or physical feelings on a 10-point scale, which can serve as a baseline of the severity of the problem.

Table 5.4　　　　A worksheet for analyzing anxiety events

Activating event	Thought	Emotion	Behavior/physical response
My reading was not fluent.	I was sure that I had left a terrible impression on Mr. Wang.	I felt extremely anxious (e.g., 10/10).	I couldn't focus my attention on the lecture. My heart beat fast (e.g., 10/10).

(3) Using socratic questions to identify cognitive distortions

Once an individual has recognized his thoughts accompanying his language anxiety, he can go on to identify the cognitive distortions included in the thoughts. Socratic questions can be employed to inquire into the thought, and identify the distortion if there is any. One may ask himself the following questions:

Is the thought a fact or an opinion?

What are the evidences supporting the belief?

What are the evidences working against the belief?

Is the conclusion based on all evidences or part of the evidences?

Is the idea confirmed/confirmable?

Is there any exaggeration in the thought?

Is there any alternative explanation for the same activating event?

How do other people view the situation?

What will be the consequence if the incident is viewed from a different perspective?

Those questions can induce a person to reflect on his own thoughts, beliefs and patterns of thinking, and discover the possible cognitive distortions.

Applying Socratic questions to the example above, the student can see that his belief that he "had left a terrible impression" on his teacher was obviously an opinion, rather than a fact. The evidence supporting this belief was only that his reading of the text was not fluent. The single evidence was too inadequate for him to arrive at a valid conclusion. In other words, the students can identify that the cognitive distortion of jumping to conclusions has been committed. An alternative realistic thought could be:

"My reading was not satisfactory, but it is nothing to be worried about. One single performance is unlikely to leave the teacher a deep impression." Such a thought is helpful, and it will probably result in a peaceful mind and positive learning behavior.

5.2.5 Practicing realistic cognitions and constructive behaviors

By challenging the maladaptive thoughts and patterns of thinking, a person is likely to find out the realistic substitutes for them.

The change of thoughts, though helpful, may not always be adequate for the effective reduction of language anxiety. For example, your cognitive distortion related to communication apprehension has been replaced by realistic thoughts, but you may still feel somewhat nervous when you are required to give a presentation in the front of the language classroom.

CBT includes not only the C (cognitive) element, but also the B (behavioral) element. Though the C element plays a dominant role, the B element is by no means negligible. A practitioner of CBT has to intentionally modify his maladaptive behaviors following the change of thoughts. A language learner needs to be actively involved in situations, events, or activities which caused him language anxiety. For example, one can volunteer to answer questions in the class, seek chances to communicate with friends or foreigners, participate in the speech contests, and so on. Practice and exposure makes a person less sensitive to pervious phobias. Similar to systematic desensitization, the behavioral change should be gradual. For instance, you can prompt yourself to volunteer to answer one question in the class at the beginning, then answer two, three, or more as time goes on.

To motivate yourself to stick to the new thought and behavior, you can use self reinforcement at the beginning stage of practice. An effective reinforcement is rewarding yourself when you think you have behaved well in the modification. There are different ways of rewarding. You may choose to watch a film, to go to the theater, to enjoy a delicious meal in your favorite dining hall, to go sightseeing, and so forth. Needless to say, improved achievement and proficiency are also great rewards.

5.2.6 Various ways of benefiting from CBT

CBT can be carried out in various ways. You may select to join a training group, to consult a therapist/counselor/professional, or to teach yourself with the help of available resources.

If you are receiving CBT under the guidance of a therapist for control of your language anxiety, you need to contact the therapist once a week or once every 2 weeks. The treatment varies from 5 to 20 sessions, with each lasting for a half or one hour. During the sessions, you must cooperate with the therapist, and honestly report to him your problems and progress. The therapist will help you to identify the maladaptive cognitions and behaviors, and design a plan for you to overcome them. You will usually be given homework (e.g., practicing the new beliefs and behaviors, or writing journals).

With the development of IT technology, computerized and internet-delivered CBT resources have come into being. Computerized CBT delivers CBT through an interactive computer interface and/or the internet. Currently, the combination of artificial intelligence and Computerized CBT has been available, which can simulate face-to-face CBT sessions. Smartphone app-delivered CBT is another new method, which employs smartphone applications to provide self-help or guided CBT. There are also CBT courses to cater the needs of different individuals.

5.3 Summary in Chinese

行为疗法和认知行为疗法是应对语言焦虑的常用策略。最典型的行为疗法是系统去敏，它是基于操作性条件反射的行为治疗技术，也称渐进式暴露疗法。其目的是帮助个体通过逐渐暴露于恐惧刺激来克服个人对刺激的敏感性，直到刺激物不再引起任何焦虑。系统脱敏治疗涉及三个阶段。第一阶段是构建焦虑刺激等级序列。其操作步骤包括：（1）列出所有可能引起同一类焦虑的刺激；（2）根据其可能诱发的焦虑水平，给各个刺激赋予等级编号；（3）按照编号，从低焦虑刺激到高焦虑刺激，将所有项目排成一个梯状序列。第二阶段是学习放松技术，如深度呼吸、意象引导、正念冥想、渐进肌肉放松等。第三阶段是建立放松与焦虑刺激的关联。由于相互抑制，放松和焦虑不可能在个人身上同时存在。当一个刺激与放松关联后，它将脱离与焦虑的关联。为建立关联，练习者需通过放松练习进入松弛和舒适状态，然后尝试想象或面对焦虑刺激等级序列中最低的项目。如果感到焦虑，个人需暂时放弃尝试，并通过放松活动获得平静，然后重试。当个人对这个刺激没有焦虑时，即可继续想象或面对序列中下一个更高的项目。通过这种方式，个人终将对所有项目不再敏感，包括序列中最高的焦虑刺激，从而完成系统脱敏。

认知行为疗法（CBT）是通过改变适应不良的认知（思想）和行为来应对语言焦虑等心理问题的心理疗法。按照CBT模型，事件引起认知反应，认知反应会进一步引起情绪和行为反应。这些因素会相互影响，形成循环过程。适应不良的思想（认知扭曲）会导致语言焦虑。认知扭曲主要有：心理过滤、全有或全无的想法、过度概括、草率推论、灾难化后果、僵化要求、情绪推理等。进行CBT治疗时，个人需要熟记这些认知扭曲的类型，意识到自己的思想不同于客观事实，学会捕捉、挑战和替换认知扭曲，并在现实中巩固合理化的认知和积极行为，从而克服语言焦虑。

Chapter 6　Design of a psychoeducation lecture for language anxiety

　　Language anxiety is very common among language learners and users. Except serious cases, most individuals do not need help from a therapist. In other words, language anxiety is a sub-clinical psychological problem for many people. On the campus, psychoeducation through a lecture, a short course, and so on, can be convenient and feasible for helping a large number of students cope with language anxiety. This chapter gives a description of an example psychoeducation lecture based on REBT, which has been used by the author for university students. Needless to say, adaptation is indispensable to make it work for a particular group of audience.

6.1　Rationale and components of the psychoeducation lecture

6.1.1　The rationale

　　A psychoeducation lecture is a cost-effective means for helping a large audience suffering from the same psychological problems. Speaking anxiety (SA) is a type of emotional problem for many language learners. The dysfunctional beliefs on language learning and using are to a certain extent responsible for learners' speaking anxiety. REBT, a psychotherapy based on modifying irrational beliefs, seems to be one of the optimum techniques to address the problem.

　　REBT, however, provides only the general principles rather than specific answers to emotional problems, which may have a variety of roots. In other words, it can not be adopted directly. Even in clinical settings, a therapist has to adapt it to the specific troubles of each client. Foss & Reitzel (1991) also suggested that specific techniques for language anxiety need to be adapted to the characteristics of the second language classroom.

6.1.2 The components

If the learners are informed of the concept of SA, the seriousness of SA, the roots of SA, and the remedies for SA, they are likely to change their SA. The psychoeducation lecture follows these assumptions and includes 4 components: (1) the prologue, (2) the background knowledge, (3) the roots and remedies of SA, and (4) the epilogue. The prologue provides a contrast of some anecdotes calling for attention: sharply different consequences resulting from extremely similar events. Succeeding the anecdotes is a brief revelation of the deep root— it is the perspective that people take that mattered. Moreover, the relationship of the events with anxiety is pointed out. The prologue ends with a short list of topics to be covered in the whole lecture. The background knowledge focuses on two topics: the concept of SA and the negative consequences of SA. The pervasiveness of SA and the incompatibility between SA and the College English Objective in China are also tapped. The purpose of this section is to help the audience not only to recognize the issue of SA, but also to attach great importance to it. The part of roots and remedies of SA includes two sub-components: (a) the SA rooted in unfeasible goals and its remedy, and (b) the SA rooted in irrational beliefs and its remedy. The "(b)" is composed of a discussion of (1) the A-B-C personality theory, which attributes anxiety to irrational beliefs; (2) a case analysis, which demonstrates how irrational beliefs cause anxiety; and (3) irrational and rational beliefs related to classroom speaking performance, which are discussed in the C-D-E pattern (Comparing the Beliefs, Disputing on the Rationality, and Examining the Consequences). The epilogue summarizes the lecture and provides strategies for the substitution and consolidation of beliefs. Here is a simplified figure demonstrating the structure of the lecture based on the script (Figure 6.1).

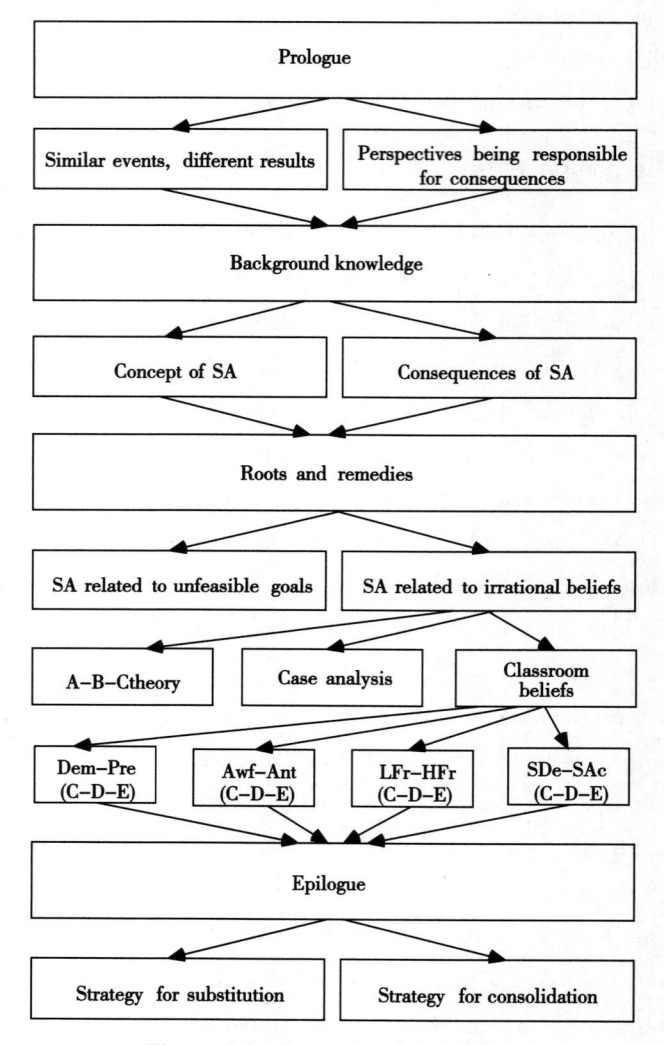

Figure 6.1 Structure of the lecture

(Dem-Pre=demands vs. full preferences; Awf-Ant=awfulizing vs. anti-awfulizing; LFr-HFr = low frustration tolerance vs. high frustration tolerance; SDe – SAc = self-depreciation vs. self-acceptance)

6.2 Script of the psychoeducation lecture

6.2.1 Prologue

Hello everyone. Welcome to the lecture. The topic for today is the roots and remedies of speaking anxiety. The purpose of the lecture is to foster the development of second language skills. First let's examine some anecdotes or facts which call for deep thought.

On March 19, 2008, a 22-year-old college graduate in Wuhan, China, was reported to have committed suicide in a lake, just because he had been suspected of pirating in his bachelor thesis. Did it deserve committing suicide? We may feel confused, but it was a logical choice for the graduate. Just a few years ago, a professor at one university discovered his paper being pirated by a professor in another university and prosecuted him, demanding 10 Fen to be paid for the pirating. A great commotion was caused in the academic circle in China. The prosecuted, however, did not commit suicide. Being unable to continue his career in the old place, he came to work in a new university. Why? It was a logical choice for the professor. There was a high school student, who failed to be admitted by a first level university in 2006, missing the cut-off score by only a few score points. To realize his dream of entering a first level university, he prepared for another year. In stead of improving, he did much worse at the second time, missing the cut-off score by tens of score points on the test. The unexpected consequence was to a great extent due to the fact that during the 3 days of admission tests in the second year, the student was sleepless every night, feeling too much pressure. Was it necessary to feel so? According to the logic of the student, the high pressure was unavoidable. There are many other students who are not outstanding in the class, but they never feel so much pressure on important tests, and can always show their best. Why? Their behavior is also logical.

According to Epictetus, a stoic philosopher, what troubles people is not an event but the perspective people take to it. We may add another statement: what frees people from the bothering of an event is also the perspective people take to it.

All the anecdotes or facts discussed above are related to the presence or absence of anxiety, which has been triggered by the perspectives taken by the concern. Anxiety not only influences our life, but also our work, especially language learning. Today we will talk about the anxiety related to foreign language speaking performance. The lecture is composed of the concept of speaking anxiety, the relationships of speaking anxiety to speaking performance, and the roots and remedies of speaking anxiety.

The remedies to be introduced by the lecture can help you overcome your psychological problems not only related to your speaking performance, but also related to other aspects of your work and your life.

6.2.2 Background knowledge

(1) Concept of speaking anxiety

Now I would like to invite you to make a self introduction in the front of audience here. Volunteers, please put up your hands (followed by a pause of approximately 30 seconds). Those who dare not put up their hands are likely to be experiencing anxiety. Anxiety is the apprehension indirectly connected with an object or objective. The anxiety involved in speaking performance is speaking anxiety. The following statements are all symptoms of speaking anxiety:

a. I tremble when I know that I'm going to be called on in my English class.

b. I start to panic when I have to speak English.

c. I always feel that the other students speak English better than I do.

d. I feel very self-conscious about speaking English in front of other students.

e. I am afraid that I will make grammar mistakes in my speaking.

All those statements signify the presence of speaking anxiety.

(2) Relationships of speaking anxiety to speaking performance

Speaking anxiety affects oral communication. It has been discovered that anxiety is negatively correlated with Language Class Sociability (LCS), the tendency to use the target language for socialization; and that anxiety is negatively correlated with Language Class Risk-Taking (LCR), the tendency to take risks when using the target language (Liu & Jackson, 2008).

It was also reported that the more anxious students produced shorter self-descriptions which were judged as lower in fluency, lower in sentence complexity, and less of the second language accent. They tended to speak with more frequent pauses and breaks, more unnecessary repetitions and more false starts (Djigunović, 2006; MacIntyre & Gardner, 1994b).

The influence of speaking anxiety on speaking performance can be demonstrated by a story. The first time being in Moscow, a Russian learner always felt that his Russian was inadequate until one day he unexpectedly found that his Russian was surprisingly fluent. A clerk annoyed him and he quarreled with the clerk. The angrier he was, the more violently he quarreled, and the more fluently he spoke Russian.

The reason was simple. The Russian learner was not worried about the grammar, the pronunciation, the words, and so on in the quarrel. With a freer mind, he could thus speak better.

Anxious individuals divide their attention between task relevant thinking (the thinking indispensable for performing a task, for example, processing the language information in communication) and task irrelevant thinking (the thinking which contributes little to performing the task, for example, the worry about the accent in communication). The efficiency of behavior is reduced as a result of the decreased cognitive resources. Moreover, anxious language learners are less likely to participate in speaking practice, which may result in poor speaking skills, leading to a higher anxiety and a vicious circle.

Speaking anxiety is a pervasive phenomenon. In Beijing, more than one-third of university students were discovered to experience speaking anxiety. In Jiangsu, a lot of middle school students were found to show serious speaking anxiety. In Taipei, school pupils were noticed to have speaking anxiety. The new College English Objective in China is to develop the integrated competency, with particular stresses on speaking and listening skills. Speaking anxiety thus hinders the realization of the essential section of the College English Objective.

6.2.3 Speaking anxiety rooted in unfeasible goals and its remedy

(1) Unfeasible goals and anxiety

Now imagine you are standing under a peach tree. There are peaches of various sizes and heights. The bigger, the higher. What could be your emotional reaction, if you are driven to pick the peaches beyond your reach? Most likely, you will experience anxiety. The primary factor responsible for your anxiety is the goal. When the goal is beyond your reach, you have lower confidence in obtaining it. The lower confidence implies a higher estimation of failure, which poses a greater threat to your personal value. Anxiety could be aroused when personal value is threatened. Most of the speaking anxiety experienced by language learners can be attributed to the excessively high goals of performance. The high goals originate from the formal classroom language learning. During the process of learning, learners listen to standard speeches, read perfect texts, and have all kinds of written and oral practice to guard against mistakes. In the long run, learners may form the idea that they are expected to use standard or perfect forms of language (the goal) and that imperfect or non-standard forms of language are forbidden or unacceptable. Anxiety may result from the awkward predicament if the learners believe that the goal is beyond their reach and what is within their reach is forbidden or unacceptable.

(2) Selecting feasible goals to control anxiety

To control your anxiety, you have to select feasible goals. You are unlikely to experience anxiety if you select the peaches which are within your reach. In the same way, you are unlikely to experience speaking anxiety if you are encouraged to speak what you are capable of speaking.

To select feasible goals, you have to interpret the concept of GOAL in a new way. Generally speaking, there are two categories of goals, the short term goals, and the long term ones. So far as the learning of a foreign language is concerned, the long term goal is to develop the competence to speak the perfect or standard language. To achieve the long term goal, you can set a series of short term goals, which are like a flight of stairs, gradually leading you to the destination. In other words, imperfect or non-standard uses of the language can be your short term goals, which can help you to approach the long term goal step by step. Let's take the learning of Chinese as a first language for an instance. "Wǒ chī fàn (I have meal)" is a simple sentence. But no one is born with the competence to speak it. At the early stage of speaking, a normal infant can only utter a single word, for example, "Fàn (Meal)". Months later, it can say a two-word sentence, such as "Chī fàn (Have meal)". It cannot say the multiple-word sentence "Wǒ chī fàn (I have meal)" until much later. With further learning, the child may gradually be able to speak more and more complicated sentences, such as "Wǒ xiǎng chī fàn (I want to have meal)" and "Wǒ xiànzài xiǎng chī fàn (I want to have meal now)".

In the learning of a foreign language, you have to consider your present stage of development, and set your own goals for speaking performance so that they are achievable with an effort. You have to bear in mind the following when deciding on your goals.

Firstly, simple or non-standard forms of speech, such as isolated words, phrases, or broken English are acceptable, and can be very communicative. Once you are abroad, you would find how useful those non-standard forms are. Here are some examples. In the dining hall, if you are thirsty, simply look at the waiter and utter one word "Water!" and you will be served; if you are hungry, utter the word "Rice!" and you will get it; if you want to go to the toilet, say the word "WC", and you will be guided to it. Do not be constrained by the language rules in routine communications.

Secondly, your speaking skill may not develop in step with your listening or reading skills. You may be capable of understanding complicated language structures in your listening or reading practice, but can only speak very simple utterances. Generally, language production skills lag behind the comprehending skills. It is quite reasonable for you to have a modest speaking goal though you may have an excellent listening or reading competence.

To overcome anxiety, please adapt your goals to your present levels. If you can use isolated words, speak them; if you can use phrases, speak them; if you can speak broken English, practice it. At different levels and stages of development, let's cherish the same courage and self-confidence, and we will succeed in grasping the second language sooner or later.

6.2.4 Speaking anxiety rooted in irrational beliefs and its remedy

Now let's discuss the second category of causes of anxiety, irrational beliefs. To achieve a better understanding of the relationships between irrational beliefs and anxiety, we have to look at a basic theory which explains the roles of beliefs in our emotional and behavioral reactions to events in our life.

(1) A—B—C personality theory

Let's suppose you are required by your English teacher to give an oral presentation, and you have the following beliefs.

I extremely wish to give an excellent oral presentation, but this is not an absolute "must" for me. If I fail to do an excellent job, it is certainly bad, but not the end of the world.

When you have such beliefs, you are unlikely to experience unduly high anxiety.

Now let's suppose again that you are required by your English teacher to give an oral presentation, and you have the following beliefs.

I must give an excellent oral presentation. If I fail to do an excellent job, it will be extremely terrible.

When you have such beliefs, you may have unduly high anxiety, which, in return, is likely to worsen your presentation. The key point here is, when you are faced with the same event, different beliefs result in different emotional and behavioral consequences, as is what the "A—B—C personality theory" is all about.

A — the activating event experienced by an individual;

B — the belief cherished by an individual for "A";

C — the emotional/behavioral consequence.

Usually, people tend to consider that "A" causes "C". Ellis, however, did not think in this way. He insisted that, in most cases, it is the "B" that directly causes the "C".

(2) Beliefs and anxiety: A case analysis

What beliefs cause anxiety? According to experts, the stiff, rigid and extreme beliefs, or irrational beliefs are responsible for most of our anxiety. The following case analysis can help us get to know how irrational beliefs lead to anxiety.

A foreign student was studying for a Ph. D. degree in English in America. He felt anxious every time he had a conference with his supervisor, because he thought that he mustn't make mistakes when speaking English with his supervisor. He thought that mistakes would prove him a stupid person. The more he thought in these ways, the more anxious he felt, and the more mistakes he tended to make. What could be the roots of his troubles?

According to the A—B—C personality theory, irrational beliefs could be the roots. The first belief held by the student was that he mustn't make mistakes when speaking English with his supervisor. This was irrational. Mistakes are unavoidable for anyone speaking any language. Here is a story. A Chinese learner of English met an American on an airplane and had a chat with him.

"What's your wife?" asked the Chinese.

"She don't work." answered the American.

"She don't work?" repeated the Chinese in surprise.

"No, she do not." answered the American indifferently.

The correct use is "does not", rather than "do not". The Chinese learner had expected native speakers of English to speak perfect English and was surprised at the grammar mistake, while the American was indifferent about it due to its commonness.

To further convince yourself, you can make a recording of the speech of your friend in the mother tongue and submit it to language experts for analysis, and you will find how frequent mistakes are. They are so common that we have got used and lost sensitivity to them.

In the above mentioned case, the student's demand that he mustn't make language mistakes was therefore irrational, and caused his anxiety.

The second belief held by the student was that making mistakes would prove him a stupid person, which was irrational, too. The intelligence of a person includes many different dimensions. According to Gardner (1983), there are 7 types of intelligence (Table 6.1).

Table 6.1　　　　　　　　　　Types of intelligence

Intelligence type	Capability and perception
Linguistic	words and language
Logical-mathematical	logic and numbers
Musical	music, sound, rhythm
Bodily-kinesthetic	body movement control
Spatial-visual	images and space
Interpersonal	other people's feelings
Intrapersonal	self-awareness

The student in the case selected only speaking performance to depreciate the whole self, having committed the fallacy of judging the whole from a part. This irrational idea was another root of his problem. What could be the remedy for his troubles?

Since anxiety originates from irrational beliefs, substituting rational beliefs for irrational ones can be expected to control or reduce anxiety. Suppose the student's beliefs were changed as "I prefer not to make mistakes when speaking English with my supervisor, but this is not a must. Mistakes would not prove me a stupid person. It just proves that I am a person capable of making mistakes, and it is on certain specific occasions that mistakes occur." Would his high anxiety continue to exist? It is unlikely.

(3) Irrational vs. rational beliefs related to speaking performance

In the second language classroom situations, 4 types of irrational beliefs could exist, according to the REBT theory by Dryden (2001): demands, awfulizing beliefs, low frustration tolerance beliefs, and self-depreciation beliefs, with demands being the core. Corresponding to the irrational beliefs, there are 4 types of rational substitutes: full preferences, anti-awfulizing beliefs, high frustration tolerance beliefs, and self-acceptance beliefs, with full preferences being the core. The irrational and rational beliefs are to be discussed in pairs. In the discussion, we will follow the "C—D—E" pattern (Compare the beliefs, Dispute on the rationality, and examine the consequences).

a. Demands vs. full preferences

Compare the beliefs. "Demands are rigid ideas that people hold about how things absolutely must or must not be" (Dryden, 2001, p. 4). For example:

I must follow the rules when I speak English.

I must speak with standard pronunciation.

I must answer the English questions perfectly.

My language teacher must give me positive evaluations.

My friends mustn't scorn me for my speaking performance.

Demands like these are irrational and at the very core of most of our speaking anxiety. The healthy substitutes for demands are full preferences. "Full preferences are flexible ideas that people hold about how they would like things to be without demanding that they have to be that way" (Dryden, 2001, p. 4). For example:

I want to follow the rules when I speak English, but I don't have to do so.

I want to speak with standard pronunciation, but it is not a must.

I want to answer the English questions perfectly, but I can answer them imperfectly.

I want my language teacher to give me positive evaluations, but unfortunately he doesn't have to do so.

I want my friends not to scorn me for my speaking performance, but unfortunately they can scorn me.

Full preferences like these are rational and at the very core of most of our healthy psychological responses to events related to speaking performance.

Dispute on the rationality. Why are full preferences rational, and demands irrational? A full preference has two obvious parts, the "partial preference" ("PP") and the "denial of demand" ("DD"), both being flexible. For example:

I want to speak correctly ("PP": flexible), but it is not a must ("DD": flexible).

A full preference is rational because the flexible "PP" can logically lead to the flexible "DD".

A demand seems to have only one part, but actually it has two parts, with one logically implied. For example, when you say you must have lunch immediately, others can logically infer that you want to have lunch immediately. The two parts of a demand are the "implied partial preference" ("IPP") and "demand" ("D"), with the former being flexible, and the latter inflexible. For example:

(I want to speak correctly ("IPP": flexible), so I must speak correctly ("D").

A demand is irrational because the flexible "IPP" can not logically lead to the inflexible "D". The discussion can be demonstrated by the following figure (Figure 6.2).

```
                              Rational    ┌─────────────────────────────┐
┌─────────────────────────┐  ─────────→   │ Full preference (flexible): │
│ (Implied) Partial       │                │ but I don't have to do so.  │
│ preference (fexible):I  │                └─────────────────────────────┘
│ want to speak correctly,│                ┌─────────────────────────────┐
└─────────────────────────┘  ─────────→   │ Demand (inflexible):        │
                              Irrationa    │ so I must speak correctly.  │
                                           └─────────────────────────────┘
```

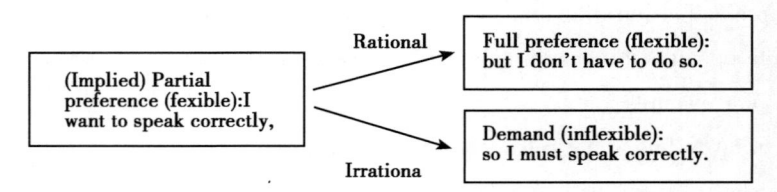

Figure 6.2 The logic of demands and full preferences

Examine the consequences. Which are beneficial, and which are detrimental? Demands are *detrimental*. They are unfeasible. Learners holding demands will experience unduly high anxiety in the language classroom, since they are aware of the possible frustrations. To avoid the occurrences of frustrations, they will try any means to avoid speaking in the group, such as escaping the classes, or refusing to volunteer answers. The ultimate result is a failure in learning a language. Full preferences are *beneficial*. On the one hand, full preferences can provide learners with enough motivation to work for the desired result; on the other hand, full preferences are unlikely to threaten learners with frustrations. Full preferences bring about peaceful mind, active class participation, risk-taking in speaking, and ultimate success in learning.

b. Awfulizing beliefs vs. anti-awfulizing beliefs

Compare the beliefs. "Awfulizing beliefs are extreme ideas that people hold as derivatives from their demands when these demands aren't met" (Dryden, 2001, p.5). They are irrational. For example:

I must follow the rules when I speak English and it's terrible if I don't.

I must speak with standard pronunciation and it's awful if I don't.

I must answer the English questions perfectly and it's the end of the world if

I don't.

My language teacher must give me positive evaluations and it's dreadful when he doesn't.

My friends mustn't scorn me for my speaking performance and it's fearful when they do.

The healthy substitute for an awfulizing belief is an anti-awfulizing belief. "Anti-awfulizing beliefs are non-extreme ideas that people hold as derivatives from their full preferences when these full preferences aren't met" (Dryden, 2001, p. 5). They are rational. For example:

I want to follow the rules when I speak English, but I don't have to do so. It's imperfect if I don't follow the rules, but not terrible.

I want to speak with standard pronunciation, but it is not a must. If my pronunciation is not so standard it's undesirable, but not awful.

I want to answer the English questions perfectly, but I can answer them imperfectly. It is unsatisfactory when my answer isn't perfect, but not the end of the world.

I want my language teacher to give me positive evaluations, but unfortunately she/he doesn't have to do so. When my language teacher doesn't give me positive evaluations it's really unfortunate, but not dreadful.

I want my friends not to scorn me for my speaking performance, but unfortunately they can scorn me. It's uncomfortable when they scorn me, but not fearful.

Dispute on the rationality. Why are awfulizing beliefs irrational, and anti-awfulizing beliefs rational? An awfulizing belief is extreme. The person believes at the time one or both of the following:

"nothing could be worse" (Dryden, 2001, p. 5);

"no good could possibly come from this bad event" (Dryden, 2001, p. 5).

Both of the ideas are irrational. Robinson's mother once told her son that everything in life was possible to become worse from the moment he was born till he lied in the coffin (Nie, 2009). Learners with awfulizing beliefs tend to enlarge the seriousness of common things: whatever is unwelcome (undesirable, unsatisfactory, unpleasant, imperfect, etc.) is awful (fearful, dreadful, terrible, disastrous, etc.). The absolute view of badness is also irrational, according to dialectics. In language learning, we can benefit from our imperfect performance. Experts regard the imperfect second language as an intermediate language, which is different from either the native or the target language. Normally, a second language learner will improve his/her intermediate language gradually until it is the same as the target language. The fact that you are speaking imperfectly reflects the truth that you are making progress normally. Even negative reactions from others are beneficial, because they can help you to become aware of the imperfect aspects of your speaking performance. An anti-awfulizing belief is non-extreme. The person believes at the time one or more of the following: "things could always be worse" (Dryden, 2001, p. 5); "good could come from this bad event" (Dryden, 2001, p. 5).

Both of the ideas are rational, because they are in sharp contrast with the irrational ideas cherished by learners with awfulizing beliefs.

Examine the consequences. Which are detrimental, and which are beneficial? In the language classroom, awfulizing beliefs are detrimental. Learners with such beliefs will experience unduly high anxiety because they can perceive the existence of various "disasters". To avoid the occurrences of the "disasters", the learners with awfulizing beliefs will try all means to avoid speaking in the group, which ultimately will result in failure in learning. Anti-awfulizing beliefs are beneficial. Learners with such beliefs perceive no "disasters" and are free from the corresponding anxiety. They are likely to participate in class interaction, taking risks in speaking, and achieve success in the end.

c. Low frustration tolerance beliefs vs. high frustration tolerance beliefs

Compare the beliefs. "Low frustration tolerance beliefs are extreme ideas that people hold as derivatives from their demands when these demands aren't met" (Dryden, 2001, p. 6). They are irrational. For example:

I must follow the rules when I speak English and I can't bear it if I don't.

I must speak with standard pronunciation and it's intolerable if I don't.

I must answer the English questions perfectly and I can't stand it if I don't.

My language teacher must give me positive evaluations and it's unbearable when she/he doesn't.

My friends mustn't scorn me for my speaking performance and I can't tolerate it when they do.

The healthy substitute for a low frustration tolerance belief is a high frustration tolerance belief. "High frustration tolerance beliefs are non-extreme ideas that people hold as derivatives from their full preferences when these full preference aren't met" (Dryden, 2001, p. 6). They are rational. For example:

I want to follow the rules when I speak English, but I don't have to do so. When I don't follow the rules it's uncomfortable to bear, but I can bear it and it's worth bearing.

I want to speak with standard pronunciation, but it is not a must. When my pronunciation is not so standard it's really unpleasant to tolerate, but I can tolerate it and it's worth it to me to do so.

I want to answer the English questions perfectly, but I can answer them imperfectly. It is not easy to accept when my answer isn't perfect, but I can accept it and it's to my best interests to do so.

I want my language teacher to give me positive evaluations, but unfortunately she/he doesn't have to do so. When my language teacher doesn't give me positive evaluations it's really disagreeable to bear, but I can bear it and I can benefit from bearing it.

I want my friends not to scorn me for my speaking performance, but unfortunately they can scorn me. It's indeed hard to tolerate when they scorn me, but I can tolerate it and it does me good to tolerate it.

Dispute on the rationality. Why are low frustration tolerance beliefs irrational, and high frustration tolerance beliefs rational? A low frustration tolerance belief is extreme. The person believes at the time one or both of the following:

"I will die or disintegrate if the frustration or discomfort continues to exist" (Dryden, 2001, p. 6);

"I will lose the capacity to experience happiness if the frustration or discomfort continues to exist" (Dryden, 2001, p. 6).

Both ideas are irrational. In the learning of a second language, rarely have any cases been reported that a learner died, became spiritually disintegrated, or lost the capacity to experience happiness merely due to an imperfect speaking performance or the negative reactions from others to the imperfect speaking performance. Even though an individual claims he/she cannot tolerate a certain event, he/she is actually tolerating it when the event has occurred. Learners with low frustration tolerance beliefs tend to consider whatever is hard/unpleasant/uncomfortable to tolerate to be intolerable.

A high frustration tolerance is non-extreme. The person believes at the time one or more of the following:

"I will struggle if the frustration or discomfort continues to exist, but I will neither die nor disintegrate" (Dryden, 2001, p. 6);

"I will not lose the capacity to experience happiness if the frustration or discomfort continues to exist, although this capacity will be temporarily diminished" (Dryden, 2001, p. 6);

"the frustration or discomfort is worth tolerating" (Dryden, 2001, p. 6).

All those ideas are rational because they are in sharp contrast with the irrational ideas held by learners with low frustration tolerance beliefs. High tolerance does not mean without attempt to change the situation. On the contrary, it suggests that a learner will improve his/her performance gradually without being annoyed by temporary imperfection. Moreover, the imperfection is worth tolerating, because the learner can benefit from it in one way or another.

Examine the consequences. Which are detrimental, and which are beneficial? Low frustration tolerance beliefs are detrimental. When learners believe that they can not tolerate the imperfect speaking performances or the possible negative reactions to their performances from others (some of which may only be their personal illusions), they will experience unduly high anxiety because those events are unavoidable in language classes. To prevent the occurrences of those events, they may try various means such as escaping language classes, or refusing to participate in interactions or volunteer speaking, which may ultimately result in failure in learning a language. High frustration tolerance beliefs result in a peaceful mind, active class participation, and risk-taking in using the unfamiliar target language. Just as a driver can keep going in the right direction with reference to the outside world, learners who are tolerant of negative feedback as well as positive feedback can achieve a better understanding of their weakness and strength so as to timely adapt their learning behaviors and avoid going in the wrong direction. High frustration tolerance beliefs may bring about a high efficiency of learning and the ultimate success in grasping the new language.

d. Self-depreciation beliefs vs. self-acceptance beliefs

Compare the beliefs. Self-depreciation beliefs are extreme ideas about oneself that people hold as derivatives from their demands when these demands aren't met. They are irrational (Dryden, 2001). For example:

I must follow the rules when I speak English and it proves me a stupid learner if I don't.

I must speak with standard pronunciation and it suggests my language aptitude being low if I don't.

I must answer the English questions perfectly and it means I'm a poor student if I don't.

I must get positive evaluations from my language teacher and it indicates that I'm valueless when I don't.

I mustn't be scorned by my friends for my speaking performance and it proves me a fool when I am scorned.

The healthy substitute for a self-depreciation belief is a self-acceptance belief. Self-acceptance beliefs are non-extreme ideas that people hold about themselves as derivatives from their full preferences when these full preferences aren't met (Dryden, 2001). They are rational. For example:

I want to follow the rules when I speak English, but I don't have to do so. If I don't follow the rules it doesn't prove me a stupid learner. I'm only a person, like everyone else, capable of failing to follow the rules in speaking performance.

I want to speak with standard pronunciation, but it is not a must. If my pronunciation is not standard it doesn't suggest my language aptitude being low; it just suggests that my pronunciation is not perfect in the present stage of my learning.

I want to answer the English questions perfectly, but I might answer them imperfectly. When my answer isn't perfect it doesn't mean I'm a poor student. I am just a person, like everyone else, capable of failing to answer questions perfectly.

I want to get positive evaluations from my language teacher but it's not a must. When I don't, it doesn't indicate that I'm valueless since I can get positive evaluations on other occasions.

I want my friends not to scorn me for my speaking performance but unfortunately they can scorn me. It doesn't prove me a fool when I'm scorned because I can be admired on other occasions.

Dispute on the rationality. Why are self-depreciation beliefs irrational, and self-acceptance beliefs rational? A self-depreciation belief is extreme. The person believes at the time one or more of the following:

"a person can legitimately be given a single global rating that defines their essence and one's worth is dependent upon conditions that change" (Dryden, 2001, p. 7) (For example: My worth goes up when I perform well, and goes down when I don't);

"you can legitimately rate a person on the basis of his or her discrete aspects" (Dryden, 2001, p. 7).

A self-depreciation belief is irrational. Firstly, an individual is a complicated whole, possessing many different aspects. If we use the lower case "i" for part of the self, and the upper case "I" for the whole self, then the upper case "I" contains many lower case "i", but the lower "i" does not equal the upper "I". The upper "I" can not be judged from a lower "i" (Figure 6.3).

Secondly, one's performance is dependent on conditions, but one's worth is stable. The stable worth cannot be evaluated by the changing performance. Self-depreciating beliefs are fallible because they define the whole self by part of the self, and evaluate the stable essence of a person by the changing conditions. A self-acceptance belief is non-extreme. The person believes at the time one or more of the following:

A person cannot legitimately be given a single global rating that defines

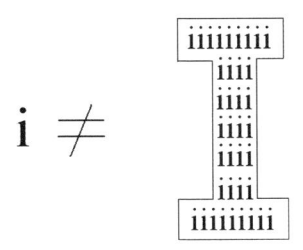

Figure 6.3 Relationship between a part and the whole

one's essence;

One's worth is not dependent upon conditions that change (Dryden, 2001, p. 7) (One's value remains the same however one performs);

It makes sense to rate discrete aspects of a person, but it does not make sense to rate a person on the basis of these discrete aspects (Dryden, 2001).

The self-acceptance beliefs are rational due to the sharp contrast with the self-depreciating beliefs.

Examine the consequences. Which are beneficial, and which are detrimental? Self-depreciation beliefs are detrimental. In the language classroom speaking performance is seldom perfect, and negative reactions to the performance from others may exist (some of which are only one's illusions). Learners with such beliefs will experience unduly high anxiety because they perceive that their personal values are always likely to be threatened. To protect their personal values, those learners will try all methods to avoid classroom interactions, which ultimately leads to a failure in learning a language. Self-acceptance beliefs, on the contrary, will bring about a peaceful mind, active participation and success in learning.

6.2.5 Epilogue

Now that you have a full understanding of the issue of speaking anxiety, the next step is to control it and change your destructive behavior in the language class. You have to select appropriate goals or criteria for your performance. If you can use isolated words, speak them. If you can use phrases, speak them. If you can use simple sentences, speak them. If you can use complicated structures, speak them. You can benefit from whatever you speak.

You should substitute rational beliefs for the irrational ones. The following sections demonstrate strategies which can be followed to foster the substitution and consolidation of beliefs.

(1) Strategy for belief substitution (Based on Dryden, 2001)

Firstly, list the speaking anxiety problems suffered by you.

I tremble when I know that I'm going to be called on in my English class.

I am afraid that the other students will laugh at me when I speak English.

...

Secondly, conduct the belief substitution.

First, select a specific example of your problems.

"*I tremble when I know that I'm going to be called on in my English class.*"

Note: All the problems you listed cannot be solved simultaneously. They should be dealt with one by one. So you have to select a specific example to begin with.

Second, describe the activating event which causes your emotional problem (A).

I'm going to be called on in my English class.

Note: The "A (activating event)", if not clear to you, can be identified by a miraculous question: what event can remove or obviously reduce your undesired physical or emotional reaction? The opposite event could be the "A". For example:

— What event can stop or obviously reduce my trembling?

— I'm NOT going to be called on in my English class.

Therefore, *I'm going to be called on in my English class* is the "A".

Third, recognize the undesired consequences (C).

a. Emotional consequence: *anxiety*.

b. Behavioral consequence: *avoiding eye contact with the teacher or sitting in the back row in the future in an attempt to reduce the probability of being called on*.

c. Learning consequence: *failure in language learning*.

Note: There are three types of "C (consequence)", the emotional (fear, worry, apprehension, shyness, etc. are all symptoms of anxiety), the behavioral, and the learning "C". The former two are dependent on your direct reactions to "A", while the last one is the long term effects likely to be caused by "A".

Fourth, recognize your irrational beliefs and their rational substitutes (B), and fill the Table (Table 6.2).

Table 6.2　　　　**Irrational beliefs and their rational substitutes**

Demand *I must give a satisfactory answer.*	Full preference *I prefer to give a satisfactory answer, but it's not a must.*
Awfulizing belief *It is extremely terrible if my answer is unsatisfactory.*	Anti-awfulizing belief *If my answer is unsatisfactory, it is indeed bad, but not so terrible.*
Low frustration tolerance belief *I cannot tolerate providing unsatisfactory answers.*	High frustration tolerance belief *Unsatisfactory answers are indeed hard to tolerate, but I can tolerate them, and they are worth tolerating, because they can teach me something.*
Depreciation belief *If my answer is unsatisfactory, it will prove that I am a stupid language learner.*	Acceptance belief *Even if my answer is unsatisfactory, it cannot prove that I am a stupid language learner. It only proves that I am an individual who is capable of giving unsatisfactory answers, and it is on this specific occasion that I give an unsatisfactory answer.*

Note: You can discover your beliefs (actual or potential) through inner dialogue as well as your knowledge about irrational and rational beliefs. A helpful question is: "Why do I have 'C' (emotional or behavioral) when I'm faced with 'A'?" The answer can reveal at least one of your irrational beliefs, based on which you can infer the other beliefs (actual or potential) with your relevant knowledge. For example:

— Why do I have anxiety when I know that I'm going to be called on in my English class?

— I am afraid I can not give a satisfactory answer.

Therefore, *I must (should, ought to) give a satisfactory answer* is the demand, based on which you can infer other beliefs with your knowledge.

Fifth, select your demand and another central irrational belief which causes your undesired emotional and behavioral reaction to "A", and simultaneously select your full preference and another suitable rational belief and fill Table 6.3 with the two groups of beliefs (You can address them *primary unhealthful beliefs* and *primary healthful beliefs*).

Table 6.3   Unhealthful and healthful beliefs

Primary unhealthful beliefs	Primary healthful beliefs
I must give a satisfactory answer. It is extremely terrible if my answer is unsatisfactory.	I prefer to give a satisfactory answer, but it's not a must. If my answer is unsatisfactory, it is indeed bad, but not so terrible.

Note: In the present case, it is hypothesized that "*It is extremely terrible if my answer is unsatisfactory*" is your most strongly felt belief besides your demand.

Sixth, set your emotional, behavioral, and learning goals (decide on your desired reactions and consequences to "A").

a. Emotional goal: *being without anxiety*

b. Behavioral goal: *having eye contact with the teacher or sitting in the front row in the future so as to increase the probability of being called on*.

c. Learning goal: *success in language learning.*

Note: The goals are dependent on your personal preference.

Seventh, Select a group of beliefs from "Table 6.3" which can better help you to realize the desired reactions and consequences to "A".

I prefer to give a satisfactory answer. But it's not a must. If my answer is unsatisfactory, it is indeed bad, but not so terrible.

Please follow the script to conduct belief substitution for your other emotional problems (homework).

(2) Strategy for belief consolidation

To consolidate the desired beliefs, you have to put them into practice. The following table is designed to help you to achieve the purpose. Please keep the table in your English text books, and fill it in according to the directions.

Historical record of your belief substitution

Direction: Please fill in one row of the following table (Table 6.4) at the end of each English class for a succession of 4 times. You are required to provide the date of the class, and to indicate (with Yes or No) whether you have recited your primary healthful beliefs before/during the class, and whether you have experienced the desired emotional/behavioral reactions during the class.

Table 6.4　　　　　　　　**Worksheet for belief consolidation**

Date	Reciting healthful beliefs		Experiencing desired reactions	
	Before class	During class	Emotional	Behavioral

6.3　Summary in Chinese

心理教育是治疗语言焦虑的一种常用形式。本节介绍的心理教育讲座设计依据的是理性情绪行为疗法（REBT），它主要包括四个部分：（1）开场白；（2）背景知识；（3）口语焦虑的根源和对策；（4）总结。

开场白部分介绍了一些值得注意的逸闻，它们涉及类似的事件，却引发不同的后果。其根源在于人们看待问题的视角不同。对于相同的事件，不同的看法会引起不同的情绪和行为反应。

背景知识部分聚焦于口语焦虑的概念及其消极影响，同时也强调了口语焦虑的普遍性，以及口语焦虑和英语教学目标的不相容性，旨在引起学生对问题的重视。

口语焦虑的根源和对策部分包括两个主要模块：（1）目标脱离现实导致的口语焦虑及其疗法；（2）非理性信念导致的口语焦虑及其疗法。第一模块介绍了调整个人目标的方法，并强调了容忍不完美表达的重要性；第二模块着重解释了非理性信念引起焦虑的原理（A—B—C 人格理论），进行了非理性信念导致焦虑的案例分析，并列举了课堂中焦虑学生经常持有的典型非理性信念。

总结部分概括了前述内容，并提出了巩固合理化信念的自我强化策略。

Chapter 7 Study of the effect of psychoeducation lecture on speaking anxiety

This chapter presents an empirical study of the effect of REBT-based psychoeducation lecture on speaking anxiety. It begins with the methodology, which covers the research questions, research variables, population and samples, instruments and materials, research design, research procedure, techniques for data analysis, and pilot studies. Following the description of the methodology, the data analysis and results corresponding to each question are presented. Finally come the discussion and conclusion to the empirical study.

7.1 Methodology

7.1.1 Research questions

In this empirical study, the following research questions are to be answered:

(1) To what extent do students experience speaking anxiety (SA) in the English language classroom? Does the SA experienced by students differ significantly in terms of gender?

(2) How is SA related to trait anxiety (TA), unwillingness to communicate (UTC), speaking self-efficacy (SSE), language class risk-taking (LCR), language class sociability (LCS), and language achievement (LA)?

(3) Can the Psychoeducation Lecture developed on the basis of the REBT reduce students' SA? Does the effect differ significantly in terms of gender?

(4) Can the Psychoeducation Lecture reduce students' speaking state

anxiety (SAstate)? Does the effect differ significantly in terms of gender?

(5) Can the Psychoeducation Lecture improve the speaking performance (assessed by the total number of words in communication units (CUs), the percent of the total number of words in mazes, and the total number of dependent clauses)? Does the effect differ significantly in terms of gender on any of the criteria? If yes, on which criterion/ criteria?

Research Question 4 was not a primary concern of the present study. It was used as a means of triangulation for Research Question 3, because theoretically speaking, the answers to Research Question 3 and 4 are consistent. The variables involved in both of the questions are closely related.

7.1.2 Research variables

A variable is a property which can take two or more values. Variables can be classified in different ways for different purposes. The following sections discuss the variables with regard to the research questions in the present study.

(1) Variables related to Research Question 1

Two variables were involved in Research Question 1: the level of SA and gender. The level of SA was used as a variable because the author wanted to examine how seriously students were suffering from anxiety related to speaking performance in the classroom. The results were helpful for understanding other findings of the present study. In other words, the level of SA functioned as a kind of background on which other findings were obtained. Gender was also considered as a variable so that the relationship between SA and gender could be discovered.

(2) Variables related to Research Question 2

Besides the SA, the TA, UTC, LCR, LCS, LA, and SSE were also involved in Research Question 2. Those variables had been found to be related to language anxiety by earlier studies. Unfortunately, none of the relevant studies had examined all the variables simultaneously, to the knowledge of the present author. Therefore, Research Question 2 filled a gap in the study of language anxiety. The significance of examining all those variables simultaneously was that the complicated relationships among them could be revealed. The discovery of the relationships might further result in pedagogical implications for the prediction and control of SA.

(3) Variables related to Research Question 3-5

Research Question 3 - 5 were to be answered by the results of an experiment, the variables involved in which are to be discussed in terms of independent, dependent, and control variables.

a. Independent variables

In an experiment, independent variables refer to the variables whose effects on other variables are to be studied. The present research involved two independent variables, the condition of experiment and gender.

The condition of experiment is the condition which a participant experiences. To test the effects of the Psychoeducation Lecture, two levels of the condition of experiment were required, one was the treatment condition in which the Psychoeducation Lecture was present, and the other was the control condition which was similar to the treatment condition except that the Psychoeducation Lecture was absent.

Gender was a factor of interest in many studies related to language anxiety. It was selected as an independent variable in the present study, so as to examine whether or not the effects of the Psychoeducation Lecture differed significantly in terms of gender. The results could help people to achieve a better understanding of the Psychoeducation Lecture.

b. Dependent variables

In an experiment, dependent variables refer to the variables on which the effects of the independent variables are to be studied. The present research involved several dependent variables: SA, SAstate, the total number of words in CUs, the percent of the total number of words in mazes, and the total number of dependent clauses.

SA was selected as a dependent variable since speaking seems to be the most important cause of language anxiety (MacIntyre, 1999). The effect of the Psychoeducation Lecture on SA was worth investigation.

SAstate was selected as a dependent variable because it could provide a triangulation for the effect of the Psychoeducation Lecture on SA. SA was a tendency to experience anxiety, while SAstate was the momentary arousal of anxiety. The tendency was believed to influence the arousal. If the Psychoeducation Lecture was effective for the SA, it should be effective for the SAstate. SAstate was not used as a means of triangulation for Research Question 1 and 2 because they were to be answered with data from surveys. SAstate can not be measured in surveys. It can only be aroused by specific tasks in specific situations, which were created by the condition of experiment related to Research Question 3-5 in the present study.

The total number of words in CUs, the percent of the total number of words in mazes, and the total number of dependent clauses were all indicators of speaking performance. Examining the effects of the Psychoeducation Lecture on those dependent variables had two merits. Firstly, it could provide a test of the causal relationship between anxiety and performance. The logic was that if the reduction of SA/SAstate resulted in an improvement of performance, it could be reasonably inferred that anxiety did influence performance. In other words, anxiety was not merely a side effect. Secondly, it could reveal which aspect of performance was influenced by anxiety.

c. Control variables

LA was likely to be related to the dependent variables in the present study. Higher achievers were hypothesized to have lower levels of language anxiety and to produce better speaking performances (Phillips, 1992; Wilson 2006). To avoid the possible influence of LA, indicators of LA (LAE and LAF) were selected as control variables, the effects of which were removed with ANCOVA.

d. Logical framework of the variables

The logic framework of the variables in the experiment is demonstrated in Figure 7.1. Indicators of speaking performance refer to the total number of words in CUs, the percent of the total number of words in mazes, and the total number of dependent clauses. The variables on the left (independent and control variables) were hypothesized to influence the variables on the right (dependent variables).

```
┌─────────────────────────┐         ┌─────────────────────────┐
│ Condition of experiment │────────▶│ SA                      │
└─────────────────────────┘   ╲ ╱   └─────────────────────────┘
                               ╳
┌─────────────────────────┐   ╱ ╲   ┌─────────────────────────┐
│ Gender                  │◀────────│ SAstate                 │
└─────────────────────────┘   ╲ ╱   └─────────────────────────┘
                               ╳
┌─────────────────────────┐   ╱ ╲   ┌─────────────────────────────────┐
│ Indicators of LA        │────────▶│ Indicators of speaking performance│
└─────────────────────────┘         └─────────────────────────────────┘
```

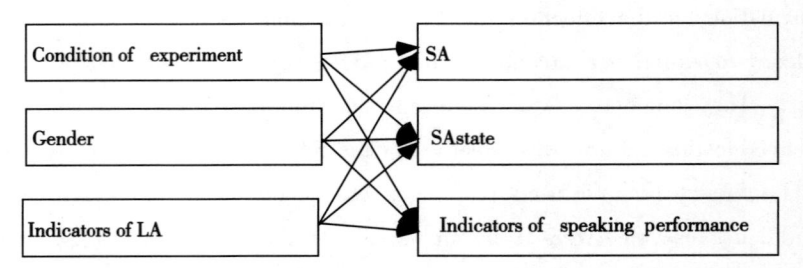

Figure 7.1 Logical framework of the variables in Research Question 3-5

7.1.3 Population and samples

(1) Characteristics of the population

The population was the first year, non-English-major students who were studying for a bachelor's degree in Guizhou College of Finance and Economics. First-year students were selected as the target population because the Psychoeducation Lecture was hypothesized to have lasting positive effects on language learning, and it was expected to benefit the learners for a longer time if the Psychoeducation Lecture was applicable to and effective for the first year students.

Students in the population were studying in the School of Maths and Statistics, the School of International Economics, the School of Finance, the School of Industrial and Commercial Management, the School of Accounting, the School of Information, the School of Public Management, the School of Resources and Environment Management, the School of Management Science and Engineering Management, the School of Culture Dissemination, the School of Law, the School of Traveling Management, the School of Education Management, the School of Economics, the School of Finance and Taxation, and the School of International Finance. They were all enrolled in the course of English as a second language, which was compulsory and credit-bearing. Four hours was regularly devoted to English every week during the first two years of college study. Students were encouraged to spend extra time in the self-regulated learning center, where they could use digital resources. The teachers here were generally Chinese. Communicative teaching approach was popularly employed.

There were about 60 students in a class.

(2) Sampling methods

A sample is a subset of the research population. Sampling refers to the procedure of obtaining the sample. Generally speaking, researchers cannot or will not study the whole population. Only one or more unit (s) of the population is/are to be actually involved in the study. To rationally select the unit (s), sampling techniques need to be employed.

Two types of sampling can be identified, the probability sampling and non-probability sampling. In probability sampling, the researcher can specify the probability of each sampling unit's being included in the sample in a single draw from the population, while in non-probability sampling, there is no way of specifying each unit's probability of being included in the sample (Frankfort-Nachmias & Nachmias, 1996).

Frankfort-Nachmias and Nachmias claimed that researchers do use non-probability samples, though they can make accurate estimates of the population's parameters only with probability samples. They suggested that non-probability sampling is employed for convenience and economy, or when the population cannot be accurately defined, or when a list of the units of the population is unavailable.

In the present research, the probability and non-probability sampling were both employed. For Research Question 1 and 2, administration of questionnaires were required. The corresponding samples were drawn with the probability sampling technique, because (a) a list of members of the population was available, and (b) no obstacles were expected to prevent the administration of a questionnaire to a random sample from the population. Probability sampling has several major forms:

a. Simple random sampling: a probability sampling procedure, in which all members of the population have an equal and independent chance of being included in the sample.

b. Stratified sampling: a probability sampling procedure, in which the sample is randomly drawn from a number of strata of the population.

c. Cluster sampling: a probability sampling procedure, in which natural clusters of the population are randomly drawn and included in the sample.

d. Systematic sampling: a probability sampling procedure, in which sample is drawn by taking every kth case from a list of the population.

For Research Question 1 and 2, the present study employed cluster sampling, because (a) the members in the population existed not only as individuals but also as natural groups (clusters), and (b) it was more convenient for the administration of the questionnaires to clusters than to isolated individuals.

For Research Question 3–5, non–probability sampling was employed, because a 14 days, experiment was to be done. It was unfeasible to randomly draw a sample, in which all the members were willing to participate in the long experiment. There are three major types of non-probability sampling techniques (Ary et al., 2006):

a. Convenience sampling: a non-probability sampling procedure, in which cases available are used for a study.

b. Purposive sampling: a non-probability sampling procedure, in which cases judged as typical or representative of the population are chosen for a study.

c. Quota sampling: a non-probability sampling procedure, in which typical cases from diverse strata of a population are selected for a study.

The present study selected convenience sampling, because the participation in the study depended on the willingness of the students, rather than the selection of the author. Volunteers were recruited by an invitation letter (see Appendix E) from the population for the study. Volunteers were ever employed as participants by other similar studies. To investigate the effects of two types of relaxation trainings on students' state and trait anxiety, Rasid, and Parish (1998) used volunteers as participants. In the study of the effects of language anxiety on cognitive processing in the second language, volunteers were employed by MacIntyre and Gardner (1994b). MacIntyre et al. (1997) also employed volunteers as subjects when studying the role of anxiety in self-ratings of second language proficiency.

(3) Sample sizes

The size of a sample is decided by taking into consideration of various factors such as the financial resources or the time available, the requirement on the accuracy of the study, the homogeneity or heterogeneity of the population on the variable (s) being studied, the requirement of statistical analysis, the size of the population (if it is a finite one), the type of study, the availability of the participants, and the sampling method, etc.

For the investigation related to Research Question 1, the sample size was 240 students (112 males, 128 females) from 5 natural groups randomly selected from the population. The size was well above the minimum requirement of 96.04, which was calculated from the following formula for infinite population (Khaimook. K., lecture on statistics, July 8, 2008):

n = ($z^2 \times s^2$) / d2

n: sample size

z: z value

s^2: variance of scores on speaking anxiety

d: maximum error

The "z" value was set as 1.96. The "d" value for the mean score on every item of the scale involved was set as 0.20 (5% times of the range of possible scores on one item — with a minimum score being 1, and the maximum score being 5). The "s^2" was set as 1 (the square of 1/4 times of the range).

For the investigation related to Research Question 2, the sample size was 103 (29 males, 74 females) from 2 natural groups. The size was also larger than the minimum requirement (96.04). It was smaller than the sample size for Research Question 1 because the questionnaire to be used for Research Question 2 was much longer, and would cost much more time to answer. To keep the sample size slightly above the minimum requirement, the author wanted to reduce the total cost of time of the learners.

For the experiment related to Research Question 3-5, the original sample size was 40 (20 males, 20 females), but only 32 (16 males, and 16 females) finished the whole experiment (The reported reasons for the attrition included visiting relatives, going shopping, and being busy with the lessons). The participants were volunteers recruited from 4 groups. The size was based on a consideration of a rule of thumb, a literature review and the purposes of the study. For experimental studies, Borg and Gall suggested 15 subjects per group as a rule of thumb (as cited in Mertens, 1998, p. 270). Rasid and Parish (1998) reported an experimental study on the effects of two types of relaxation trainings, in which 55 subjects were distributed in three experimental conditions. Jones (2002) put a total sample of 43 participants in four experimental conditions in a study related to cognitive restructuring and relaxation training. In an experimental study on language anxiety and language processing, which involved the measurement of language-specific state anxiety, Djigunovic (2006) employed 33 participants, who were assigned to two experimental conditions. Arnold (2007) assigned a sample of 56 participants to three experimental conditions to study the effects of communication trainings on speaking anxiety. The above experiments involved variables similar to the present research. They employed 16.06 participants/subjects in one experimental condition on an average. Compared with the rule of thumb and the average size of sample in one experimental condition found in the literature review, the actual sample size of 32 for the present experiment (with 16 in each experimental condition on an average) was large enough.

The gender distribution of the sample was demonstrated in Table 7.1 (Originally, the 20 males and 20 females were equally and randomly assigned to both groups).

Table 7.1　　Gender distribution of the sample in the experiment

	Control group	Treatment group
Male	7	9
Female	8	8

The control group was part of the sample that experienced the control condition, and the treatment group was that experienced the treatment condition. As was clear, females were evenly distributed in both the treatment and the control group, while two more males were involved in the treatment group than in the control group. The distribution was approximately balanced.

7.1.4　Instruments and materials

The following instruments and materials were employed for measuring the variables involved in the study, as well as recruiting the participants. All the scales were adapted or adopted from instruments applicable to college students (Horwitz et al., 1986; Liu, & Jackson, 2008; Djigunović, 2006).

(1) Speaking Anxiety Scale

It was a 15-item 5-point Likert scale, of which 13 items were adapted from the FLCAS (Horwitz et al., 1986; the FLCAS was not adopted because it measures more than merely speaking anxiety), and 2 were developed by the present author. The items were all supposed to measure SA. In the adaptation, the specific term of "English" or "English class" replaced the general term of "foreign language" or "(foreign) language class" so that the new scale was more appropriate for the present study with the English language learners. The developed items were "9. I feel relaxed when I am speaking English in the class" and "12. I feel relaxed when the English teacher asks questions that I have not prepared for in advance". They were employed because most of the adapted items were supposed to examine the degree of the presence of SA, rather than the absence of it. In the adaptation of the items from the FLCAS and the development of the new items, the author made reference to Arnold (2007), who had adapted and developed similar items in his study involving the measurement of foreign language Communication Apprehension (anxiety in oral communication) with the US university students. Following each item were 5 choices for measuring the construct of SA: (A) Strongly Agree; (B) Agree; (C) Undecided; (D) Disagree; (E) Strongly Disagree. The choices were scored 1, 2, 3, 4, 5 respectively if the relevant item was a symptom of the absence of the construct measured, and scored 5, 4, 3, 2, 1 if was the presence. Higher scores indicated higher levels of the construct. The Chinese version of this scale was used in the study (Appendix A).

(2) Trait Anxiety Scale

It was a 10-item 4-point Likert scale, adapted from the trait scale of the State-Trait Anxiety Inventory (Spielberger, 1983). The adaptation was based on a pilot study (See Pilot Study A in section 7.1.8), in which the trait scale had been found to have two principal components: the worry dimension and the mood dimension. It was the mood dimension that was judged as significantly correlated with speaking anxiety. To save the time of the participants, the present study adapted the original trait scale in such a way that only the 10 items which had loadings over 0.40 on the mood dimension were selected and composed the Trait Anxiety Scale. Following each item were 4 choices: Not At All; Somewhat; Moderately So; Very Much So. The scoring rules were similar to those for the "Speaking Anxiety Scale", except that only 4 grades were available. The Chinese version of this scale was used in the study (Appendix B: Part 1 (I)).

(3) Unwillingness to Communicate Scale

It was a 20-item 5-point Likert scale adopted from Burgoon (1976). The scale has two principal components: the approach – avoidance dimension (UTCA), which is measured by the first 10 items on the scale, and the reward dimension (UTCR), which is measured by the last 10 items on the scale. According to Burgoon and Koper (as cited in Liu and Jackson, 2008), the former represents an individual's tendency to avoid or take part in interpersonal or small group communications (signifying the presence or absence of CA), while the latter reflects one's attitudes toward communication—whether one considers it to be a valuable, sincere, and personally favorable activity or feels socially isolated and views communication as a dishonest, manipulative, or unbeneficial activity. The choices and the scoring rules were the same as those for the "Speaking Anxiety Scale". The Chinese version of this scale was used in the study (Appendix B: Part One (II)).

(4) Language Class Risk-Taking Scale

It was a 6-item 5-point Likert scale adapted from Ely (1986). The word Spanish in the original scale was changed to English to suit the English learners in the present study. The choices and the scoring rules were the same as those for the "Speaking Anxiety Scale". The Chinese version of this scale was used in the study (Appendix B: Part Two (II 1-6)).

(5) Language Class Sociability Scale

It was a 5-item 5-point Likert scale adapted from Ely (1986). The adaptation, choices, and scoring rules were the same as those for the "Language Class Risk-Taking Scale". The Chinese version of this scale was used in the study (Appendix B: Part Two (II 7-11)).

(6) Speaking Self-Efficacy Scale

It was a 7-item 5-point Likert scale. Six of the items were adapted by the author from the self-rating scale for speaking ability, attached to the College English Requirements (general) (http://www.edu.cn/20040120/3097997.shtml). The original scale requires ticking the items which suit the learner, while the present author adapted it into a 5-point Likert scale. One of the items was developed by the author: "The integrated level of my English speaking ability was __". This item was intended to examine the overall self rating. Following each item were five choices: 1, 2, 3, 4, 5, with "1" for the lowest rating, and "5" for the highest rating on the dimension described. Higher scores indicated higher degrees of SSE. The Chinese version of this scale was used in the study (Appendix B: Part Three).

(7) Speaking State Anxiety Scale

It was an 8-item 5-point Likert scale directly adopted from Djigunović (2006), who used the scale to investigate the speaking state anxiety ("language-specific state anxiety", p. 197) of the "Croatian L1-English L2" (p. 195) undergraduates. In the present study, it was used for both the pre- and posttest of the SAstate. On the posttest, an additional item "English score on college entrance test __" was present to investigate the language achievement on College Entrance Test (LAE). The choices and scoring rules were the same as those for the "Speaking Anxiety Scale". The Chinese version of this scale was used in the study (Appendix C).

(8) Speaking performance assessment criteria

They were criteria for assessing the speaking performance in terms of the total number of words in CUs, the percent of the total number of words in mazes, and the total number of dependent clauses. The criteria were adopted from Wilson (2006), who based his criteria on Hunt (1965), Loban (1975), Larsen-Freeman (1983), Phillips (1990, 1992) (as cited in Wilson, 2006). Both Wilson (2006) and Phillips (1992) applied the criteria to assessing second language speaking performance of university students. The selection of the three criteria was determined by (a) part of the purposes of the study and (b) findings on the relationships of language anxiety to speaking performance. As part of the purposes, the study attempted to find out the effect of the Psychoeducation Lecture on speaking performance. Only the characteristics of speaking performance which were likely to be influenced by language anxiety were further likely to be sensitive to the Psychoeducation Lecture. Research findings (Phillips 1992; Wilson, 2006) suggested that the three criteria adopted in the present study were likely to measure aspects of speaking performance liable to the influence of anxiety. The Chinese version of this scale was used in the study (Appendix D).

(9) Invitation letter

To recruit volunteers for the experiment, an invitation letter was prepared, and read by the present author at the beginning of English classes to students to be sampled from the population. The letter primarily covered the purposes, requirements, and general procedure of the study. Issues which could influence the willingness of participation were also included in the letter. The English version of this letter was used in the study (Appendix E).

(10) Pictures for oral description

Two pictures were needed for oral description in order to test the speaking performance, with one for the pretest (Picture A), and the other for posttest (Picture B). To select the pictures, the author first prepared ten similar ones downloaded from the internet, and then displayed them on the big screen in the front of a multimedia classroom before a sample of ten students randomly drawn from the research population. From the ten pictures, the students were required to evaluate and select two which they thought were appropriate for testing their speaking performance and were approximately equivalent in difficulty. Based on the tendency of selections of the ten students, two pictures were finally chosen as being appropriate for use and approximately equivalent in difficulty. Both pictures were scenes of life in schools. For actual use in the experiment, the pictures were printed by a color printer on papers of size A4.

(11) Psychoeducation Lecture

It was a lecture of approximately 1 to 1.5 hours, which primarily focused on dysfunctional beliefs related to English speaking performance. The script was developed from the REBT (Dryden, 2001). When the preliminary script was completed, a voiced PowerPoint lecture was created on it and shown to a group of 5 college students for evaluation. Based on their suggestions, the author improved the voiced PowerPoint lecture, and submitted it to 5 experts for examination. They all approved to its validity. A pilot study (See Pilot Study B in section 7.1.9) also supported the effectiveness of the lecture for the reduction of SA. It was then that the lecture was decided to be employed in the main study for further examination (the script in Chaptered 6 is a version improved after the main study). The lecture was delivered in Chinese with the help of PowerPoint (See Appendix F for the script).

(12) Indicators of language achievement

Language achievement (LA) was indicated by the language achievement on College Entrance Test (LAE), and the language achievement on Final-Term Test (LAF). The two indicators were expected to well reflect the construct of LA.

7.1.5 Research design

Research Question 1 entailed a survey, in which the Speaking Anxiety Scale was administered to all the participants, investigating their levels of SA and demographic variables with gender included.

Research Question 2 also entailed a survey, in which the Questionnaire on Disposition and Learning was administered to all the participants, investigating their levels of TA, UTC, SA, LCR, LCS and SSE. As indicators of LA, LAE was required to be reported on the questionnaire, and LAF was collected from the English teachers concerned at the end of the term.

Research Question 3-5 entailed an experiment. An equal number of males and females were recruited. Both the males and the females were randomly and equally divided and put into the control and the treatment group. The pre-and posttest for both groups were the same, involving the measurement of SA, SAstate, and speaking performance.

The only difference in the experimental condition was that the treatment group received the Psychoeducation Lecture between the pre-and posttest, while the control group did not (Table 7.2). SA was measured by the Speaking Anxiety Scale, SAstate by the Speaking State Anxiety Scale, and speaking performance by oral description of the pictures. In addition, the indicators of LA were also investigated in similar ways to those for Research Question 2.

Table 7.2 Design for Research Question 3-5

Group	Pretest	Treatment	posttest
Treatment	SA	Yes	SA
	SAstate		SAstate
Control	Speaking performance	No	Speaking performance

The experiment took a true experimental design, since random assignment of participants was followed. Random assignment of participants is a prerequisite of typical tests of parametric statistics, according to Shaver (as cited in Mertens, 1998). Repeated measures were employed so that the gain scores on the variables could be obtained. Since the only difference in the experimental condition between the two groups was the presence or absence of the Psychoeducation Lecture, the difference in the scores gained between the two groups could be reasonably attributed to the effects of the Psychoeducation Lecture.

7.1.6 Research procedures

(1) Procedure for Research Question 1-2

To collect data for answering Research Question 1 and 2, the Speaking Anxiety Scale and the Questionnaire on Disposition and Learning was administered. The common steps for the two surveys with the questionnaires included: (a) distributing the questionnaires; (b) telling the participants the purpose of the questionnaire (for the survey related to Research Question 1, using "the purpose is to gain a better understanding of your second language learning experience"; for that related to Research Question 2, using "the purpose is to gain a better understanding of your second language learning experience and your disposition"), and promising them that the information would only be used for a study, with privacy kept; (c) giving the participants chances for questioning; (d) asking the participants to answer the questionnaires; (e) collecting the questionnaires; and (f) providing the participants means of communication for further possible inquiring.

(2) Procedure for Research Question 3-5

To collect data for answering Research Question 3 and 5, an experiment was performed. The experiment included a pretest, a treatment, and a posttest. The steps involved were as follows.

a. Pretest

The pretest measured the SA, SAstate and speaking performance individually according to the respective appointment. A participant from the control group and one from the treatment group took turns to receive the tests, which were administered in two common classrooms (Room 1 and Room 2) in succession. In Room 1, a collaborator of the author was present and he would ask each participant arrived to first answer the Speaking Anxiety Scale (Appendix A) according to the direction and then wait outside Room 2 (the next room). In Room 2, the chief examiner (the author) and a collaborator were present. The collaborator sat by a desk in the second row, manipulating a notebook computer, which was used to play the recorded directions and record the speech of the participant. On the desk in the first row right in front of the collaborator were a speaker, a picture and a pencil-box in which a pen was kept for answering the questionnaire. When a participant entered the room, the collaborator would play the recorded Chinese direction, and the participant was supposed to follow it.

"您好，请站在前边（静音5秒，其间助手用手势指示对方到放有话筒、图片和文具盒的桌子边）。请拿起话筒和图片，您的任务是用英语看图说话一分钟，您的讲话将被录音，请准备10秒钟（静音10秒）。请填写问卷（助手暂停指导语，递去口语状态焦虑量表，直到问卷填完并取回后，取消暂停）。请拿起话筒和图片，立即开始看图说话（助手启动录音。一分钟后，助手停止录音，并告诉被试者'时间到，谢谢参与'。召唤下一名被试者）。"

In English, the direction was to the meaning:

Hello! Please come and stand in the front of the room (There are 5 seconds of recorded silence, in which the collaborator gestures the participant to stand by the desk where the speaker, the picture and the pencil-box are kept). Please pick up the speaker and the picture. Your task is to orally describe the picture in 1 minute. Your description will be recorded. Please prepare for 10 seconds (10 seconds of recorded silence follows). Please answer the questionnaire (The collaborator puts the direction in pause, passes the Speaking State Anxiety Scale (Appendix C) to the participant, and waits for it to be answered. The collaborator collects the questionnaire as soon as it is finished, and cancels the pause). Please pick up the speaker and the picture, and begin the description right now (The collaborator starts the recording of the speech. When 1 minute is over, the collaborator stops the recording and announces, "Time is up, thank you for your participation". He calls the next one to enter for the test).

The whole course (in Room 2) lasted for about 5 minutes for a participant on an average.

b. Treatment

Following the pretest on the same day, the participants in the treatment group received the treatment with the Psychoeducation Lecture. The participants in the control group received no elaborate treatment.

c. Posttest

Fourteen days after the pretest was the posttest. The elaborate delay was expected to reduce the effect of the pretest, and to give the participants in the treatment group a chance for adapting their emotional and behavioral reaction to the speaking performance in the English class. The posttest was similar to the pretest, except that (a) an audience of 9 collaborators was present; (b) the picture for oral description was different; (c) the direction was slightly different (Following "Your description will be recorded（您的讲话将被录音）" (see the direction for pretest), was one additional sentence "The students will evaluate your performance（同学们将对您做出评价）"; and (d) on the Speaking State Anxiety Scale, the item "English score on college entrance test ＿" was present. Except the "（d）", which was intended to investigate the LAE, all the other measures were expected to arouse higher levels of anxiety.

7.1.7　Data analysis techniques

（1）Data analysis for Research Question 1

Research Question 1 focused on the extent of SA experienced by the learners, and the difference of SA in terms of gender. In the preliminary analysis, descriptive statistics were employed to analyze the demographic features, such as gender and age, and the reliability of the Speaking Anxiety Scale was calculated to show the internal consistency of the instrument.

Following the preliminary analysis, the minimum （Min）, maximum （Max）, mean, and standard deviation （Std.）of the levels of SA were analyzed. The mean was further judged as low, if the average score on each item of the scale （average item score） fell below 3, as moderate if between 3 and 4, and as high if above 4 （Liu & Jackson, 2008）. The percentage of the participants falling within each of the three intervals （the distribution） was also reported. Independent Samples T Test was employed to show whether the means differed significantly in terms of gender, and Chi Square Test was employed to examine whether the distributions of the levels of SA differed significantly in terms of gender.

（2）Data analysis for Research Question 2

Research Question 2 focused on the relationships of SA to other variables. The reliabilities of all the scales were analyzed in the preliminary analysis. Then, correlation was conducted to show the interrelationships between the variables, and stepwise regression was employed to examine the significant predictors of SA. Since neither the correlation nor the regression analysis could reveal the causal relationships between the variables, structural equation modeling （SEM） was conducted.

（3）Data analysis for Research Question 3-5

Research Question 3-5 aimed at examining the effects of the Psychoeducation Lecture on the SA, the SAstate, and the speaking performance. In the preliminary analysis, the speaking performance was transcribed and quantified in terms of the total number of words in CUs, the number of dependent clauses, as well as the percent of the total number of words in mazes, following the speaking performance assessment criteria (Appendix D). The reliabilities of the quantification, as well as those of the rating scales were then calculated.

Succeeding the preliminary analysis, the gain scores (posttest-pretest) of the dependent variables (SA, SAstate, the total number of words in CUs, the number of dependent clauses, and the percent of the total number of words in mazes) were computed for use in the analysis of covariance (ANCOVA). The related assumptions were:

a. Gain scores for the control group are dependent on the effects of LA (LAE, LAF) and the effects of extraneous variables;

b. Gain scores for the treatment group are dependent on the effects of the Psychoeducation Lecture, the effects of LA (LAE, LAF), and the effects of extraneous variables;

c. The effects of extraneous variables on both groups were equal.

Consequently, ANCOVA was the preferable technique for the analysis. By using the gain scores as the dependent variables, the condition of experiment as the fixed/independent variable, and treating the IAE and LAF as covariates, the effects of the Psychoeducation Lecture could be analyzed.

To further examine whether the effects of the Psychoeducation Lecture on the dependent variables differed in terms of gender, the condition of experiment and gender were both used as independent variables in the ANCOVA (with other variables remaining the same), so that the interaction effects between them could be displayed. The effects of the Psychoeducation Lecture on the dependent variables could be inferred as differing significantly in terms of gender or not according to whether the interaction effects were significant or not.

7.1.8 Pilot Study A

This pilot study was related to the examination and development of the instruments for Research Question 1-2.

(1) Purpose of Pilot Study A

The purpose was to examine (1) the reliabilities of the scales for answering Research Question 1-2, and (2) the significance of the correlations between SA and several other variables (or the principal components of the variables) to be involved in Research Question 2.

(2) Participants in Pilot Study A

The participants were 44 (13 males, 30 females, 1 without reporting gender) first year non-English majors from a natural group in Guizhou College of Finance and Economics.

(3) Instruments for Pilot Study A

The instrument was an integrated questionnaire composed of a list of scales for measuring TA, UTC (UTCA, UTCR), SA, LCR, and LCS. Except for TA, which was measured by the 20-item trait scale of the State-Trait Anxiety Inventory (Spielberger, 1983), all the other variables were measured in similar ways as those in the main study.

(4) Procedure for Pilot Study A

The Pilot study was conducted at the beginning of an English class. After distributing the questionnaire, the author told the participants that the purpose of the survey was to gain a better understanding of the relationships of English learning and disposition, and promised them the confidentiality of the information. When it was finished about 20 minutes later, the author collected the questionnaires and thanked the participants.

(5) Data Analysis for Pilot Study A

Firstly, the scales involved in the questionnaire were submitted to the analysis for the Cronbach's reliabilities. Secondly, the variables measured by the scales were submitted to the analysis for the principal components. Thirdly, Pearson correlation was conducted to examine the relationships between SA and the other variables (or the principal components of the variables).

(6) Results and Discussion of Pilot Study A

The Cronbach's Alpha yielded suggested an acceptable internal consistency for each of the scales concerned (Table 7.3). The relatively small Alpha values for the LCR and LCS (.67, .71) could be attributed to the length of the scales. Liu and Jackson (2008) achieved an Alpha value of .60 for LCR and .76 for LCS.

Table 7.3   Reliabilities of the scales employed in Pilot Study A

	TA	UTC	SA	LCR	LCS
Alpha	.88	.84	.85	.67	.71

Principal component analysis (with rotated solution) was conducted only for the TA, because (a) the two components for the UTC were known (UTCA, and UTCR: see Section 7.1.4), (b) the SA was measured by elaborately adapted items from the FLCAS, and therefore it was already a sub-scale of the FLCAS, with no need for further analysis, and (c) following related literature, the LCR and LCS could all be accepted as single-dimensioned instruments (see Liu & Jackson, 2008). The results (Table 7.4) showed that the TA had two principal components. There were 10 items having loadings over 0.40 on each of the components. Component 1 was labeled "the worry dimension", because most of the items loaded heavily on it tapped the degree of worry, while component 2 was labeled "the mood dimension", because the relevant items expressed the construct of mood.

Table 7.4   Principal components of TA found in Pilot Study A

	Component 1	Component 2
Item 5	.834	.234
Item 11	.788	-.052
Item 18	.771	.260
Item 20	.755	.132
Item 17	.747	.241
Item 9	.722	.163
Item 12	.720	.491
Item 8	.695	-.126
Item 15	.682	.008
Item 14	.529	.474

continued

	Component	
	1	2
Item 2	.390	-.037
Item 4	.365	.281
Item 3	.128	.725
Item 16	.152	.709
Item 6	.030	.694
Item 1	.032	.653
Item 13	.049	.580
Item 10	.205	.576
Item 19	.110	.553
Item 7	-.048	.506

Pearson correlation (Table 7.5) revealed that the SA was significantly correlated with the UTCA and the LCR, but not with the other variables or the principal components of the variables. Since the levels of significance of correlation coefficients are strongly influenced by sample sizes, it is plausible to hypothesize that the correlations of the SA with the mood dimension of the TA ($p = .053$) and the LCS ($p = .062$) can be significant with larger samples. Even the correlation between the SA and the UTCR ($p = .102$) can be hypothesized to be significant when the size of sample is large enough, due to the fact that Liu and Jackson (2008) ever found that they were significantly correlated. It is more plausible to consider the correlation between the SA and the worry dimension of TA to be insignificant than to be significant, because (1) the $p = .383$ is too far from being significant, and (2) no studies were found to reveal significant correlations between the two.

Table 7.5   Correlations found in Pilot Study A

		SA	TA (worry)	TA (mood)	UCTA	UCTR
TA (worry)	r	.135				
	p	.383	.			

continued

		SA	TA (worry)	TA (mood)	UCTA	UCTR
TA (mood)	r	.294	.573 (**)			
	p	.053	.000	.		
UCTA	r	.423 (**)	.399 (**)	.538 (**)		
	p	.005	.008	.000	.	
UCTR	r	.253	-.078	.183	.434 (**)	
	p	.102	.619	.240	.004	.
LCR	r	-.758 (**)	-.105	-.244	-.453 (**)	-.233
	p	.000	.499	.111	.002	.133
LCS	r	-.284	.226	-.025	-.152	-.187
	p	.062	.141	.874	.332	.229

n = 44; TA (worry) = the worry dimension of TA; TA (mood) = the mood dimension of TA; ** correlation at 0.01 (2-tailed).

(7) Conclusion to Pilot Study A

With reference to relevant literature, the pilot study suggested that the translated scales for the TA, UTC, SA, LCR, and LCS were reliable. The worry dimension of the TA was not related to SA. For the main study, all the scales were wholly applicable except the TA, from which the items measuring the worry dimension of trait anxiety should be removed, so as to avoid wasting time measuring a component unrelated to SA.

7.1.9 Pilot Study B

This pilot study was related to Research Question 3-5. It was expected to validate the Psychoeducation Lecture before it was used for the main study.

(1) Purpose of Pilot Study B

The purpose of this study was to examine whether the Psychoeducation Lecture could significantly reduce the SA.

(2) Participants in Pilot Study B

The participants were 33 (8 males, 25 females) second year English majors from a natural group in Guizhou College of Finance and Economics. Though all of them participated in the pretest and the treatment, only 23 (5 males, 18 females) of them finished the posttest.

(3) Instruments for Pilot Study B

a. Speaking Anxiety Scale

It was a 15-item Likert scale of agreement employed for the measurement of the SA (Appendix A).

b. Psychoeducation Lecture

It was a lecture of 1 to 1.5 hours on dysfunctional beliefs related to SA. The Psychoeducation Lecture used in this pilot study was the same as that used in the main study (See Appendix F for the script).

(4) Procedure for Pilot Study B

The study was composed of a pretest of SA, a treatment with the Psychoeducation Lecture, and a posttest of SA. The pretest of the SA was achieved by administering the questionnaire containing the speaking anxiety scale at the beginning of a normal English class. After distributing the questionnaires, the author told the participants that the purpose of the survey was to gain a better understanding of their experience in English learning, and promised the learners the confidentiality of the information. When the questionnaires were finished about 5 minutes later, they were collected. Succeeding the collection of the questionnaires, the author announced that a lecture was to be delivered then and immediately began the treatment with the Psychoeducation Lecture. After about 80 minutes, the treatment was over. The posttest of the SA was administered with the same questionnaire and at the same time as those for the pretest 14 days later. After the distribution of the questionnaires, the author told the participants that they were required to report their emotional and behavioral reactions to English classes since they received the lecture. The questionnaires were finished and collected after about 5 minutes and thus the posttest of the SA was completed.

(5) Data analysis for Pilot Study B

The data collected were first submitted to the analysis for the reliabilities of the scale involved, and then to Paired-Samples T Test to examine the change of the SA after the treatment.

(6) Results and discussion of Pilot Study B

Preliminary analysis yielded a Cronbach's Alpha of .90 for the speaking anxiety scale used in the pretest, and .92 for the same scale in the posttest, both indicating high internal consistencies of the scale. Paired-Samples T Test showed that: (a) the mean score (an average of the sums of the scores on all the 15 items achieved by different participants) for the posttest was smaller than that for the pretest (40.83 < 45.61: see Table 7.6), (b) the difference between the mean on the posttest and that on the pretest was significant ($t = 4.88$, $p = .000$), and (c) scores on the posttest were significantly correlated with those on the pretest ($r = .85$, $p = .000$).

The results seemed to suggest that the experiment had acceptable validity and that the reduction of the SA could be attributed to the effect of the Psychoeducation Lecture.

Table 7.6 Means of SA for pretest and posttest in Pilot Study B

		Mean	N	Std. Deviation	Std. Error Mean
Pair	Pretest	45.61	23	8.63	1.80
	Posttest	40.83	23	8.76	1.83

(7) Conclusion to Pilot Study B

This pilot study seemed to support the effectiveness of the Psychoeducation Lecture as an anxiety reduction instrument for language learners. The lecture was worth further examination in the main study.

7.2 Data analysis and results

This section covers the data analysis and results (see Appendix G for the distribution of selections on the scales). For the data analysis and results, the extent of SA experienced by the students (Research Question 1), the relationships of SA to other variables (Research Question 2), as well as the effects of the Psychoeducation Lecture on SA, SAstate, and speaking performance (Research Question 3-5) are analyzed and reported. The results of Research Question 3-5 are reported together due to the fact that the effects of the same independent variables on different dependent variables could be conveniently examined together with the same statistical techniques.

7.2.1　Results to Research Question 1

To what extent do students experience Speaking Anxiety (SA) in the English language classroom? Does the SA experienced by students differ significantly in terms of gender?

Preliminary analysis revealed that, among all the 243 participants investigated, 240 (112 males, 128 females) provided complete responses. The 3 cases with missing data were deleted in further statistical analyses. The ages reported had a mean of 19.39 years, ranging from 17 years to 24 years. The coefficient Alpha yielded was .90 which was an acceptable index of the internal consistency of the Speaking Anxiety Scale.

Following the preliminary analysis were the descriptive and inferential analyses. Table 7.7 displays the descriptive statistics of the levels of SA corresponding to the total sample, males, and females respectively. The level of SA for each participant was represented by the average score he/she got on each item (average item score: the sum of one's score on all the items divided by the number of items), and the possible range was 1 to 5.

Table 7.7　　　　　　　　　　Descriptive statistics for SA

	N	Min.	Max.	Mean	Std.
Total	240	1.40	4.67	3.04	.67
Male	112	1.47	4.60	3.03	.65
Female	128	1.40	4.67	3.04	.69

The means for different groups (3.04, 3.03, 3.04) all signified moderate levels of SA. The results of Independent-Samples T Test indicated no significant difference, t = -.17, df = 238, p = .87, in the mean levels of SA in terms of gender. The implications of the levels of SA can be demonstrated on Figure 7.2.

The mean levels of SA found in the present study suggested that both the male and the female participants selected a point slightly beyond the "Undecided" to a statement like "I do not worry about making mistakes in my

I do not worry about making mistakes in my English class.

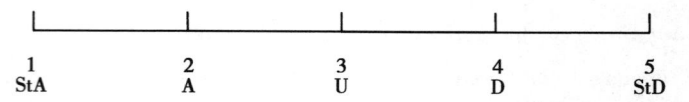

```
|_____|_____|_____|_____|
     1          2          3          4          5
    StA         A          U          D         StD
```
(StA=Strongly Agree; A=Agree; U=Undecided; D=Disagree;StD=Strongly Disagree)

Figure 7.2 Demonstration of the implications of the levels of SA

English class" on an average.

To compare the distributions of the levels of SA between males and females, the frequencies of the scores of SA falling within different intervals (see Section 7.1.7) were calculated. For the males, 53 (47.3%) fell in the low interval, 53 (47.3%) in the moderate, and 6 (5.4%) in the high interval. The corresponding statistics for the females were 62 (48.4%), 56 (43.8%), and 10 (7.8%) (Figure 7.3). Those differences did not seem to be large. The Chi-square Tests indicated no significant difference, $\dot{x}^2 = .72$, df = 2, p = .70, in the distribution of the levels of SA in terms of gender.

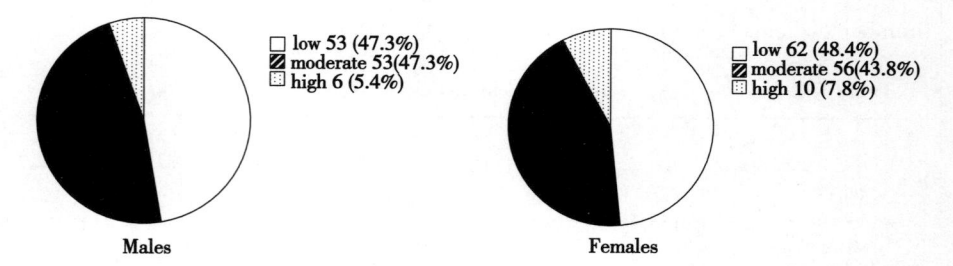

Males: low 53 (47.3%); moderate 53(47.3%); high 6 (5.4%)

Females: low 62 (48.4%); moderate 56(43.8%); high 10 (7.8%)

Figure 7.3 Distributions of levels of SA

7.2.2 Data analysis and results to Research Question 2

How is SA related to Trait Anxiety (TA), Unwillingness to Communicate (UTC), Speaking Self-Efficacy (SSE), Language Class Risk-Taking (LCR), Language Class Sociability (LCS), and language achievement (LA)?

Preliminary analysis revealed acceptable reliabilities for all the rating scales involved (Table7.8). The moderate reliabilities for LCS and LCR (.60, .66) was due to the length of the scales (5, 6 items). "Other things being equal, the longer the test, the greater its' reliability" (Ary, Jacobs, Razavieh, & Sorensen, 2006: 265). Liu and Jackson (2008) ever reported a reliability of .60 for the LCR. Anyway, all the Alpha coefficients yielded in the present study were "acceptable" "for research purposes" (Alpha >.50; see Ary et al., 2006, p. 267).

Table 7.8   Statistics related to the reliabilities
of the instruments for Question 2

	TA	UTC	UTCA	UTCR	LCR	LCS	SSE	SA
Items	10	20	10	10	6	5	7	15
Response	100	100	100	100	100	100	96.1	100
Alpha	.78	.81	.78	.84	.66	.60	.89	.89

N = 103; Items = total number of items; Response = the percent of cases with full responses.

To further reveal the relationships of the SA to other variables from different perspectives, the data were submitted to the analyses of Pearson correlation, stepwise regression, and SEM.

For correlation and regression analysis, the LA was not only represented by the two indicators (LAE, LAF), but also by the average of them (LAav = (LAE×100 ÷ 150 + LAF) ÷2. The average was calculated in this way because the total score for the LAE was 150, and that for the LAF was 100). Since the UTC was a multidimensional construct, both of the sub-components (the UTCA, and the UTCR) were all submitted to the analyses so as to achieve a precise understanding of their relationships to the SA.

Correlation analysis (Table 7.9) revealed that the SA was positively correlated with the TA, UTC, UTCA, as well as the UTCR, and negatively correlated with the LAE, LAF, LAav, LCR, LCS, as well as the SSE. The correlations suggested, on the one hand, that learners who had the tendency to experience negative mood, to avoid communication with others, or to consider communication as unrewarding, were liable to experience high SA. On the other hand, the correlations implied that higher SA was related to lower English achievement, lower tendency to use the English form whose correctness is beyond one's confidence or to use English for socialization in the classroom.

Table 7.9   Inter-correlations for SA and the other variables

	LAE	LAF	LAav	TA	UTC	UTCA	UTCR	LCR	LCS	SSE
LAF	.25*	1								
LAav	.71**	.86**	1							
TA	-.24*	-.16	-.24*	1						
UTC	-.30**	-.15	-.28**	.50**	1					
UTCA	-.17	-.13	-.20	.36**	.80**	1				
UTCR	-.31**	-.11	-.24*	.42**	.74**	.19	1			
LCR	.22*	.16	.26**	-.30**	-.41**	-.37**	-.26**	1		
LCS	-.05	-.06	-.07	-.20*	-.28**	-.26**	-.17	.27**	1	
SSE	.29**	.35**	.41**	-.31**	-.34**	-.27**	-.25*	.23*	.16	1
SA	-.29**	-.26**	-.36**	.34**	.58**	.57**	.30**	-.54**	-.33**	-.38**

N = 95103; * correlation at 0.05, ** at 0.01 (2-tailed).

To select the best model for the prediction of the SA, the variables involved in the correlational analysis were further submitted to stepwise regression analysis. The results are displayed in Table 7.10.

Table 7.10   Regression coefficients for the prediction of SA ($R^2 = .46$)

	Beta	t	p
UTCA	.42	5.251	.000
LCR	-.33	-4.029	.000
LAav	-.18	-2.332	.022

The regression model could be expressed as: SA = .42UTCA - .33LCR - .18LAav ($R^2 = .46$), suggesting that the first best predictor for SA was UTCA, the second was LCR, and the third was LAav, with 46% of the variance of SA capable of being accounted for by the predictors.

As neither the correlation nor the regression analysis could reveal causal relationships, analysis with SEM was followed. SEM is different from an experiment for examining causal relationships. In an experiment, the researcher manipulates the independent variables and observes the effects on the dependent variables, while in the SEM the researcher specifies or partly specifies one or more models based on knowledge or theories and examines whether the data support the model (s). To conduct the SEM, two preliminary steps were needed.

Firstly, construct the measurement models. The measurement models specify how the observed variables depend on the unobserved or latent variables. In the present study, the observed variables included the LAF, LAE, and all the items on the scales involved. The latent variables were the SA, TA, UTC, UTCA, UTCR, LCR, LCS, SSE, and LA. Since the UTC was not a uni-dimensional construct, it was excluded from the SEM. No information would lose, because both of its principal components (UTCA and UTCR) were present in the SEM. Except the LA, each latent variable was related to many observed variables, and parceling was in need (Zhang, Yang, Liang, Wang, & Shao, 2008). Two parcels were constructed for each latent variable, which were signified by "_ 1" and "_ 2" (for example, TA_ 1, TA_ 2: see Figure 7.4). LAE, LAF, and the parceled variables all served as indicators in the SEM. Each indicator also received the influence of an error variable (for example, e1→TA_ 1, e2→TA_ 2).

Secondly, construct the structural model, which specifies the relationships between the latent variables. The present study was more explorative than confirmative. In other words, the few relationships theoretically sound were specified by the author, as were symbolized by the thicker lines, with arrows indicating the directions of influence. Many other relationships beyond the confidence of the author were symbolized by the thinner lines, suggesting that they were suspected by the author, and were to be specified by specification search. In the structural model, the latent variables receiving the influence of other latent variables were endogenous variables, each of which received the influence of an error variable (for example, e4→UTCA). The hypothesized relationships specified by the author were:

(1) "TA→UTCA/UTCR→ SA →LCR/LCS"

TA was a tendency to experience anxiety in various situations, UTCA/UTCR was related to the tendency to experience anxiety in communication

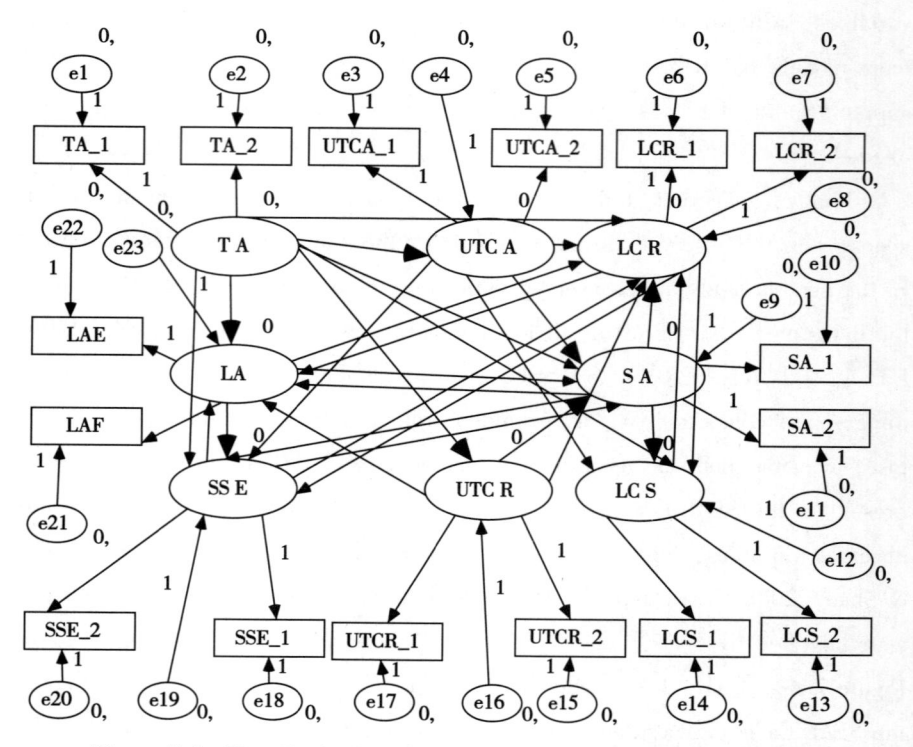

Figure 7.4　Hypothesized relationships for SA and the other variables

situations, and SA was the tendency to experience anxiety in English communication situations (language class). Therefore, the more general disposition was likely to influence the more specific disposition (deduction). SA could further influence LCR/LCS because when a learner was fearful about speaking English itself, he/she was likely to be more fearful about speaking English when the additional risks of committing mistakes existed, and was unlikely to speak English for socialization.

(2) "TA→LA →SSE"

Anxiety was likely to distract the attention or occupy the cognitive resources which could otherwise be used for learning (see Section 2.6.2). Learners suffering from anxiety were likely to have a lower efficiency of learning, and consequently a lower language achievement (LA). The LA, whether indicated by the LAE or LAF, was an objective mirror of one's level, which was likely to influence the self rating of one's level (SSE).

The hypothesized relationships to be specified by the specification search included: (a) "TA→LCR"; (b) "TA→SA"; (c) "TA→LCS"; (d) "TA→SSE"; (e) "UTCA→LCR"; (f) "UTCA→LCS"; (g) "UTCA→SSE"; (h) "UTCR→LCR"; (i) "LA→LCR"; (j) "LCR→LA"; (k) "LA→SA"; (l) "SA→LA"; (m) "SSE→LA"; (n) "UTCR→LA"; (o) "SSE→LCR"; (p) "LCR→SSE"; (q) "SSE→SA"; (r) "SA→SSE"; (s) "LCS→LCR"; and (t) "LCR→LCS". The rationale for the hypothesis was: a. personality variables (TA, UTCA, UTCR) may influence second language variables (LA, LCR, LCS, SA, SSE), rather than the reverse, because the former seem to be more fundamental than the latter; b. second language variables may have mutual influences; c. uncorrelated variables are unlikely to have significant causal relationships and should be dismissed from examination.

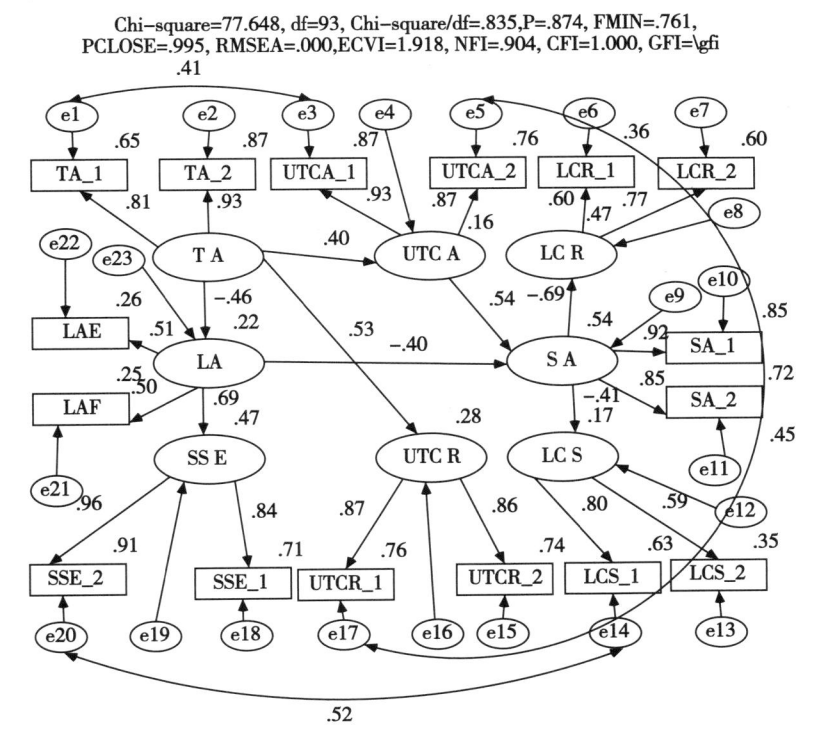

Figure 7.5 Estimated relationships for SA and the other variables (Model A)

The output of the estimation was further adjusted with reference to the fitness measures, and ultimately two satisfactory models were obtained: Model A and Model B (see Figure 7.5, Figure 7.6). The differences between them were the directions of the arrows between LA and SA, and some of the parameters.

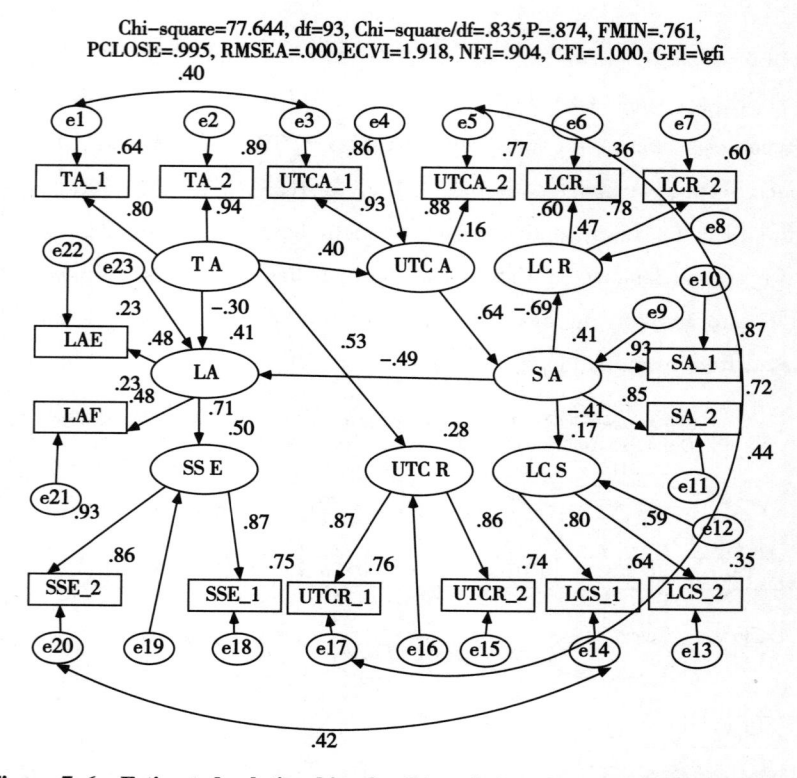

Chi-square=77.644, df=93, Chi-square/df=.835, P=.874, FMIN=.761, PCLOSE=.995, RMSEA=.000, ECVI=1.918, NFI=.904, CFI=1.000, GFI=\gfi .40

Figure 7.6　Estimated relationships for SA and the other variables (Model B)

Both models were based on standardized estimations. The directions of the single-headed arrows signified the directions of causation, with the numbers near the midpoints of the arrows representing the regression weights or direct factor effects. The double-headed arrows indicated correlations, with the numbers near the midpoints of the arrows showing the coefficients.

The regression weights and correlation coefficients all achieved statistical significance, except the coefficient between e14 and e20, which was quite near the level of significance ($p = .065$ in Model A, .062 in Model B), and plausible for being included in the model. The number near the upper right side of a rectangular or elliptical figure signified the Squared Multiple Correlation, indicating the percent of variance of the variable accounted for by the other variables directly or indirectly related to it. The fitness measures (Chi-square, df, etc.) were displayed on top of the path diagrams, all indicating acceptable goodness of fit.

Both models indicated that the SA was directly influenced by the UTCA, and it could further affect the LCR, as well as LCS. The TA had direct or indirect influences on all the other latent variables. The SSE and UTCR had no significant influence on other variables. The two models together showed that the SA and the LA had mutual influences. The Squared Multiple Correlations suggested that a total of 54% of the variance of SA could be accounted for by the directly or indirectly related variables in Model A, and 41% in Model B. Moreover, most of the latent variables were also indirectly related to each other through the intermediary of the error variables which were correlated.

7.2.3 Data analysis and results to Research Question 3-5

Research question 3 - 5 focus on the effects of the Psychoeducation Lecture:

Can the Psychoeducation Lecture developed on the basis of the REBT reduce students' SA? Does the effect differ significantly in terms of gender?

Can the Psychoeducation Lecture reduce students' Speaking State Anxiety (SAstate)? Does the effect differ significantly in terms of gender?

Can the Psychoeducation Lecture improve the speaking performance (assessed by the total number of words in Communication Units (CUs), the percent of the total number of words in mazes, and the total number of dependent clauses)? Does the effect differ significantly in terms of gender on any of the criteria? If yes, on which criterion/ criteria?

Of all the 40 students having volunteered to participate in the experiment, 32 (80%) students actually completed all the phases. The rate of attrition was not high compared with that encountered by Rasid & Parish (1998) who ever reported a two-week experiment similar to the present one, in which only 62.5% finished all the phases. The data of those who failed to complete the experiment were deleted in further analyses.

The transcription of the speaking performance was accomplished by the author, checked and improved by a peer researcher until it was believed to be satisfactory.

The quantifying of the speaking performance was conducted by the author and a peer researcher separately, following the Speaking Performance Assessment Criteria (Appendix D). Here is an example of the transcription and quantification of the recorded speech of a participant (words in normal font stand for words in CUs, in italicized font for words in mazes, and in bold font for words in CUs as well as in dependent clauses):

The Transcription

There are four boys in the picture. *We can* we can see that *two boys* two boys are discussing and two boys *look look boos* look book. *One one boys* one boys is very happy. Maybe *the book the books* the books *has has something interesting* has something interesting *to you* to he.

The Quantification

(1) The number of CUs is 4. The total number of words in CUs is 33.

a. There are four boys in the picture ·················· 1 CU

b. we can see that two boys are discussing and two boys look book ·················· 1 CU

c. one boys is very happy ·················· 1 CU

d. Maybe the books has something interesting to he ·················· 1 CU

(2) The number of mazes is 7. The total number of words in mazes is 20. The percent of total number of words in mazes is 20 ÷ (20 + 33) × 100% = 37.74%.

a. *We can* ·················· 1 maze

b. *two boys* ·················· 1 maze

c. *look look boos* ·················· 1 maze

d. *One one boys* ·················· 1 maze

e. *the book the books* ·················· 1 maze

f. *has has something interesting* ·················· 1 maze

g. *to you* ·················· 1 maze

(3) The total number of dependent clauses is 2.
  a. that two boys are discussing ·················· 1 dependent clause
  b. and two boys look book ·················· 1 dependent clause

Pearson correlations showed high inter-rater reliabilities for the quantification of speaking performance on each criterion (Table 7.11). To eliminate the inconsistencies between the raters, the ratings were further examined and revised against the criteria until agreement was arrived at on all the ratings.

Table 7.11   Inter-rater reliabilities signified by Pearson correlations

	PreCU	PreM	PreDep	PosCU	PosM	PosDep
r	.99**	.99**	1.00**	1.00**	.99**	1.00**

Pre-= Pretest of; Pos-= Posttest of; -CU = total number of words in CUs; -M = percent of total words in mazes; -Dep = total number of dependent clauses; ** correlation at 0.01 (2-tailed).

The reliabilities of the instruments for SA and SAstate were also calculated. The results showed high internal consistencies of both scales on either the pretest or the posttest (Table 7.12).

Table 7.12   Statistics related to the reliabilities of instruments for Question 3-5

	Pretest		Posttest	
	SA	SAstate	SA	SAstate
Items	15	8	15	8
Response (%)	100	100	100	100
Alpha	.94	.83	.96	.93

N = 32; Items = total number of items; Response = the percent of cases with full responses.

To examine the effects of the Psychoeducation Lecture on the dependent variables, descriptive statistics of the gain scores (posttest-pretest) of the SA, the SAstate, the total number of words in CUs, the percent of total number of words in mazes, and the total number of dependent clauses were compared between the control and the treatment group (Table 7.13). The Average Item

Scores were employed for the pre-and posttest of SA and SAstate.

Table 7.13   Descriptive statistics for the gain scores of the dependent variables

	Minimum		Maximum		Mean		Std. Deviation	
	Ctrl	Trt	Ctrl	Trt	Ctrl	Trt	Ctrl	Trt
GainSA	-.73	-1.87	.40	.13	-.14	-.57	.36	.72
GainSAstate	-.50	-2.38	.13	.38	-.14	-.64	.16	.77
GainCU	-28.00	-20.00	23.00	48.00	-3.33	14.18	14.58	16.39
GainM (%)	-33.33	-35.65	26.57	29.17	-4.00	-.37	17.71	13.89
GainDep	-2.00	-2.00	2.00	3.00	-.40	.29	1.35	1.49

Ctrl = control group; Trt = treatment group; Gain-= gain score of; see Table 7.11 for other labels.

According to Table 7.13, both the SA and SAstate had negative mean gain scores in either the control or the treatment group (-.14; -.57; -.14; -.64), which suggested the possibility of desensitization effects caused by the repeated measurements. The participants were not so anxious in the posttest as in the pretest, no matter which group they were in. But compared with the control group, the treatment group had greater absolute mean gain scores (|-.57|>|-.14|; |-.64|>|-.14|), suggesting that the SA and SAstate decreased more for the treatment group on an average. In terms of the total number of words in CUs and the total number of dependent clauses, the positive mean gain scores of the treatment group (14.18, .29) suggested that, on an average, the treatment group expressed more comprehensible speech, and used more dependent clauses in the posttest than in the pretest. In sharp contrast, the negative mean gain scores of the control group (-3.33, -.40) revealed the opposite tendency. As to the percent of total number of words in mazes, the negative mean gain scores of both groups (-4.00%, -.37%,) implied that the proportions of useless information expressed by both groups decreased in the posttest, and decreased more for the control group (|-4.00%|>|-.37%|). Those changes, as a whole, suggested that the Psychoeducation Lecture could have produced its effects, having reduced the anxiety and influenced the speaking performance.

To examine the statistical significance of the effects of condition of experiment when the possible effects of ability or LA (LAE, LAF) were controlled, ANCOVA was conducted, and the output is displayed in Table 7.14.

Table 7.14   **Effects of the condition of experiment**

Source	Depend	SS	df	MS	F	Sig	η^2
Condition of Experiment	GainSA	1.55	1	1.55	4.65	.04	.14
	GainSAstate	1.65	1	1.65	4.78	.04	.15
	GainCU	1561.09	1	1561.09	7.09	.01	.20
	GainM	452.51	1	452.51	2.69	.11	.09
	GainDep	1.57	1	1.57	.79	.38	.03

Depend = Dependent Variable; SS = Sum of Squares; MS = Mean Square; η^2 = Partial η^2.

According to Table 7.14, the condition of experiment had significant effects only on the gain scores of SA, SAstate, and the number of total words in CUs (p =.04, .04, .01), and the proportions of total variation of the three dependent variables attributable to the condition of experiment were respectively .14, .15, and .20 (see the η^2).

The descriptive and the inferential statistical results (Table 7.13, 7.14) together suggested that the Psychoeducation Lecture could reduce the SA, the SAstate, and increase the total number of words in CUs.

To further examine the effects of gender, both gender and condition of experiment were used as independent variables in the ANCOVA. The results (Table 7.15) showed no significant interaction effects on any of the dependent variables, indicating that the effects of the Psychoeducation Lecture did not differ in terms of gender.

Table 7.15   **Effects of condition of Experiment × Gender**

Source	Depend	SS	df	MS	F	Sig	η^2
Condition of Experiment× Gender	GainSA	.05	1	.05	.14	.71	.01
	GainSAstate	.04	1	.04	.11	.75	.00
	GainCU	242.90	1	242.90	1.08	.31	.04
	GainM	2.16	1	2.16	.01	.91	.00
	GainDep	.58	1	.58	.27	.61	.01

7.3 Discussion

Rating scales, indicators of LA, indicators of speaking performance, and the Psychoeducation Lecture were used in the present study. The rating scales all had acceptable reliabilities. There seemed to be no problem with the indicators of LA (the LAE was nationally used, while the LAF was used in the whole college). Adopted from repeatedly published criteria, the indicators of speaking performance were out of question. The employment of the Psychoeducation Lecture for treating SA was also theoretically justifiable. The results were consequently acceptable, and were to be discussed in the following.

7.3.1 Extent of SA experienced by the learners

The extent of SA experienced by the learners was revealed by the mean level as well as the distribution of the levels. The mean (3.04) of the total sample revealed by the present study indicated a moderate level of SA. In terms of distribution, more than half of the learners fell in the moderate or high intervals of SA.

Both the mean and the distribution revealed in the present study are worth the concern of language teachers, because they could have serious negative effects on the development of the speaking skill and speaking performance.

Firstly, SA is a barrier for the skill development. Learners suffering from higher SA are less likely to participate in class interactions (Young, 1991). The reduced chances of practice could result in a lower level of the speaking skill, which might lead to a still higher level of SA, and thus begin a vicious circulation.

Secondly, SA could have negative effects on performance. An anxious person might divide his/her attention between task relevant thoughts and task irrelevant ones. The reduced cognitive resources could result in a lower efficiency of performance. Therefore, on occasions when speaking the second language is unavoidable, the more anxious learners are likely to perform more poorly than their less anxious counterparts, even when there is no difference in the actual ability. The poorer performance may result in a more painful experience for the speaker, which could cause an even higher level of SA and lead to a vicious circulation, similar to that in the skill development.

Both of the vicious circulations deserve the attention of educators. Whether for the purpose of developing the speaking skill or improving the efficiency of performance, the issue of SA should be controlled.

The mean levels of SA, as well as the distributions, however, did not differ between males and females, a finding similar to those of some research, but different from others. Though beyond explanation, the finding is significant because it could contribute to the accumulation of facts which may ultimately lead to the clarification of the confusion.

7.3.2 Relationships of SA to the other variables

The relationships of SA to other variables were examined by means of correlation, stepwise regression and the SEM. The results of the three types of analyses, though internally consistent, reflected the relationships from different perspectives.

(1) Relationships of SA to the other variables in terms of correlation

The correlation analysis indicated that the SA was positively correlated with the TA, the UTC, the UTCA, as well as the UTCR, and negatively with the LA (signified by LAE, LAF, and LAav), the SSE, the LCR, as well as the LCS.

The directions and strengths of some of the correlations found in the present study are quite similar to those found by other studies. Table 7.16 displays a comparison of the coefficients yielded by the present study with those yielded by Liu & Jackson (2008).

Table 7.16   **Comparison of correlation coefficients for the same constructs**

Correlated factors	Present study (n=103)	Liu & Jackson (n=547)
SA (FLCAS2) ↔ UTC (UCS)	.58 **	.525 **
SA (FLCAS2) ↔ UTCA (UCS1)	.57 **	.582 **

continued

Correlated factors	Present study (n=103)	Liu & Jackson (n=547)
SA (FLCAS2) ↔ UTCR (UCS2)	.30**	.257**
SA (FLCAS2) ↔ LCR	-.54**	-.457**
SA (FLCAS2) ↔ LCS	-.33**	-.368**

Labels by Liu and Jackson were in the brackets.

The direction and strength of the correlation between TA and SA (.34**) in the present study are also similar to those between trait anxiety and foreign language classroom anxiety (.29**) found by Horwitz (1991). Those similarities seem to support the validity of the present correlational findings.

The correlations implied that learners with a higher negative mood, a stronger unwillingness to communicate with people, were likely to experience higher anxiety when speaking the second language in the classroom. The higher anxiety further suggested a lower language achievement, a lower self-efficacy in speaking ability, and a weaker tendency to take risks or socialize in the target language in the classroom.

(2) Relationships of SA to the other variables in terms of regression

Stepwise regression yielded a model: SA = .42UTCA -.33LCR -.18LAav, suggesting that the SA could be best predicted by the UTCA, LCR, and LAav. This model is extremely similar to Liu & Jackson (2008, p.81), who found that the first best predictor for SA (FLCAS2) was UCS1 (= UTCA: β = .31), the second best one was LCR (β = -.24), and the third was OE (the Overall English Proficiency, which is equivalent to the LAav: β = -.20).

The regression model indicated that language teachers could foretell the levels of speaking anxiety by the degrees of communication apprehension (UTCA), the tendencies to take risks in the language class, and the levels of language achievement.

(3) Relationships of SA to the other variables in terms of SEM

Both Model A and Model B confirmed all the original hypotheses with which the author had specified the structural model, except that about the influence of UTCR on SA. The findings also seem to be supported by other research. The influence of TA on LA is consistent with the views of Tobias and

Eysenck (as cited in MacIntyre & Gardner, 1991; 1994a), who explained the effects of anxiety on learning in terms of cognitive interference. The influence of LA on SSE is supported by MacIntyre, Noels, Clément (1997: 274), who suggested that "those who are more proficient tended to perceive themselves as more proficient". The effect of UTCA on SA can also find its echo in literature: Horwitz, Horwitz, Cope (1991: 30) insisted that "People who typically have trouble speaking in groups are likely to experience even greater difficulty speaking in a foreign language". The findings about the influences of SA on both LCR, and LCS are consistent with Samimy & Tabuse who suggested that anxiety could affect risk-taking (as cited in Matsuda & Gobel, 2004), and consistent with Young (1991) who insisted that some students may become so fearful of speaking in class that they refuse to participate at all. The insignificant influence of UTCR on SA seems to suggest that UTCR is a construct different from what was hypothesized by the author. The author hypothesized that UTCR is a tendency to experience anxiety in general communication situations, and the tendency could transfer to the second language classroom. Since the results from the SEM did not support the hypothesis, it seems that UTCR is not a general tendency to experience anxiety, though it is a tendency to have negative attitude to communication. This result from the SEM implies, for example, individuals who regard communication as a valueless behavior may not necessarily feel fearful about communication.

The findings from the SEM are significant for: (a) it provided data support for some of the claims held by researchers on the relationships between the variables involved; (b) the mutual influences between SA and LA revealed here are helpful for the clarification of the confusion concerning the relationships between the two variables (Researchers have argued about whether language anxiety is primarily a cause or effect in language learning. The present study seems to suggest that it could be both a cause and effect); and (c) the causal relationships could be used for controlling the SA.

(4) Convergence of different analyses

The variables related to SA in the present study could be put in two categories: personality features, and non-personality features. The former include UTC (UTCA, UTCR) and TA, while the latter include the LA, SSE, LCR, and LCS. The analysis of regression and SEM both suggested that SA was primarily a function of the personality feature of UTCA (among the variables involved in Research Question 2), because UTCA was found to be the best predictor of SA (Table 7.10), and UTCA had the strongest influence on SA.

7.3.3 Effects of the Psychoeducation Lecture

The effects of the Psychoeducation Lecture were examined through the experiment. The results showed that, when ability (LA) was controlled with ANCOVA, the Psychoeducation Lecture could reduce the learners SA, SAstate, and improve the speaking performance by increasing the total words in CUs. The effects of the Psychoeducation Lecture did not differ in terms gender.

To evaluate the validity of the study, the effect of the Psychoeducation Lecture on SAstate was examined as a means of triangulation. Since the effects of the model on both the SA and SAstate were found to be consistent (both types of anxiety were reduced and the degrees of reduction did not differ significantly in terms of gender), it could be reasonably inferred that the results about the effect of the Psychoeducation Lecture on SA were valid.

The results concerning the effect of the Psychoeducation Lecture on speaking performance were consistent with the common finding by Phillips (1992) and Wilson (2006), both of whom discovered that higher language anxiety was related to smaller total number of words in CUs. The results of the present study, however, were more revealing, because the findings by Phillips and Wilson were both correlational in nature, which only suggested the possible influence of language anxiety on speaking performance, while the results of the present study were based on an experiment, which provided more persuasive evidence about the influence of anxiety on performance. But the present study did not support the divergent findings between Phillips and Wilson. Perhaps unknown variables had their roles in the divergences.

The Psychoeducation Lecture was developed from the REBT (a type of CBT). The results related to the effect of the Psychoeducation Lecture on SA were inconsistent with Jones (2002), who failed to discover any significant effects of CBT (cognitive restructuring and relaxation training) on language anxiety. The different results were probably caused by (a) the technique (Jones did not develop the CBT for language anxiety, while the present author did), and/or (b) the experimental design (Jones gave the posttest immediately following the treatment and thus deprived the students of the chances to practice the desired emotional/behavioral reactions in real situations of language learning, while the present author delayed the posttest and provided the students with chances to do them).

The findings have great theoretical, as well as practical implications. Theoretically, they suggested that beliefs play a key role in SA, and that modifying beliefs could reduce SA. The findings also indicated that REBT is not only effective for use in clinical settings, but also in second language learning and using situations when appropriately adapted. Since the reduction of anxiety led to a change of the performance, the study implied that anxiety is not only a side effect of poor language learning. Practically speaking, the findings on the effects of the Psychoeducation Lecture are of great pedagogical implications.

7.3.4 A model for SA, beliefs in communication in L2, and UTCA

One more issue seemed to be in puzzle. On the one hand, the fact that the Psychoeducation Lecture could reduce SA by modifying beliefs in communication in the second language (L2) supported the inference that SA was obviously influenced by those beliefs. On the other hand, the results of stepwise regression and SEM suggested that SA was strongly influenced by UTCA. The relationships could be demonstrated by Figure 7.7. The puzzle was: What was the relationship between UTCA and beliefs in communication in L2?

To answer the question, the author advanced a hypothesized model. Similar to the influence of beliefs in communication in L2 on SA, there are beliefs in communication in general, which influence UTCA. Moreover, the beliefs in communication in general influence the beliefs in communication in L2 (see Figure 7.8; G = general).

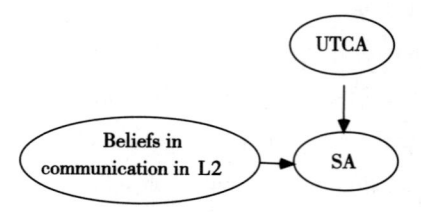

Figure 7.7 Influences of beliefs in communication in L2 and UTCA on SA

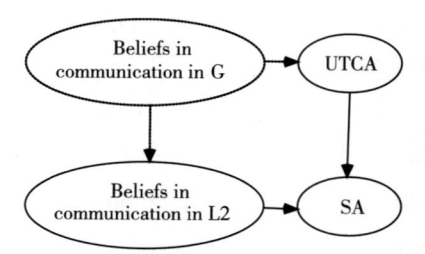

Figure 7.8 Hypothesized model connecting SA, beliefs in communication in L2 and UTCA

  The hypothesized relationships conform to logic and relevant theories. Both SA and UTCA represent the degree of fear of oral communication (in the second language or in general). If the SA is influenced by beliefs, the UTCA is equally likely to be influenced by beliefs, though the beliefs could be different, in terms of analogy. The A—B—C personality theory also supports the inference. The logic for the influence of belief in communication in general on beliefs in communication in L2 is obvious because the former subsumes the latter (deduction).

  The model also conforms to intuition. For example, if a person believes he must speak perfectly and imperfect speaking performance is terrible (beliefs in communication in general), he is likely to be afraid to express himself in a group (UTCA). Moreover, with the same beliefs, he is likely to believe that he must speak perfectly and imperfect speaking performance is terrible in the second language (beliefs in communication in L2).

  The merit for the hypothesized model is that it connects all the key variables in the present study.

7.4 Conclusion and pedagogical implications

This section primarily presents the conclusion and pedagogical implications of the study. The conclusion centers on the answers to the research questions. The pedagogical implications indicate the inferences drawn from the study which may benefit second language teaching and learning. In addition, recommendations for future studies are also briefly listed at the end of this section.

7.4.1 Conclusion of the study

The present study investigated the extent of SA experienced by the research population. The relationships of SA to the TA, UTC (UTCA, UTCR), LA, SSE, LCR, as well as LCS were examined from various perspectives. For the reduction of SA, a Psychoeducation Lecture was developed on the basis of the REBT and tested in an experiment. A survey of 240 participants was involved in the investigation of the extent of SA, 103 in the exploration of the relationships of the SA to other relevant variables, and an experiment with 32 participants was conducted for the test of the effects of the Psychoeducation Lecture. The instruments employed included a series of rating scales and the criteria for assessing the speaking performance (including the total number of words in CUs, the number of dependent clauses, and the percent of total number of words in mazes). The scales and criteria could be accepted as valid because they were all adapted or adopted from instruments employed by researchers in situations similar to the present one, and were approved by Chinese experts after examination. They could be considered as reliable due to the satisfactory or acceptable values of the coefficient Alpha and inter-rater correlations. The data were submitted to descriptive as well as inferential statistical analyses. The results support the following conclusion.

(1) The SA experienced by the learners was alarming, as can be seen by the mean and the distribution. The mean yielded in the present study suggested a moderate level of SA. Approximately half of the learners' levels of SA fell in the

moderate or high interval. In terms of gender, neither the mean nor the distribution of the levels of SA differed significantly.

(2) Complicated relationships existed between SA and the other variables. In terms of correlation, SA was positively correlated with TA, UTC, UTCA, as well as UTCR, and negatively with the LA, SSE, LCR, as well as LCS. In terms of prediction, The SA could be significantly predicted by the UTCA, LCR, and the LA. In terms of causal relationships, the SA seemed to be influenced by the TA as well as UTCA, and it could further influence LCR as well as LCS. The LA and SA had mutual influences.

(3) The Psychoeducation Lecture, developed on the REBT, was capable of reducing SA/SAstate and improving speaking performance (increasing the total number of words in CUs). The effects of the Psychoeducation Lecture on SA/SAstate and speaking performance did not differ significantly in terms of gender.

7.4.2 Pedagogical implications

The levels of SA experienced by the learners were relatively high and deserved the attention of language teachers. Since SA has negative effects on speaking performance, it is urgent to control the levels of SA. The following strategies can be tried by language teachers.

(1) Identify and predict individuals who have or are liable to have a high level of SA based on the correlates and predictors, the best of which are the UTCA, LCR, and LA. Those constructs could be gradually discerned by the language teacher as he/she gets familiar with the learners. With the help of the information on those constructs, the teacher can well identify and predict learners suffering from SA.

(2) Create a cheering atmosphere in the language classroom, because the mood dimension of trait anxiety (TA) was found to have an indirect influence on the SA. If the learners feel happy, pleasant, secure, satisfied, and contented (low TA), they are likely to experience low SA in the language classroom. Happy learners seem to be comfortable learners. Crookall & Oxford (1991) suggested that teachers can improve the classroom atmosphere by means

of games, simulations, pair work, group work, and structured exercises that change the communication pattern of the classroom. The teacher can also make the language learning an interesting and enjoyable experience by skillful uses of information technology such as the internet or multimedia techniques.

(3) Control or reduce the UTCA. The UTCA was discovered to have a direct and most important effect on the SA of all the variables involved in the present study. The UTCA signifies the degree to which learners experience communication apprehension (CA), which may have its root in beliefs, history of reinforcement or punishment, skill acquisition, and situation factors (Daly, 1991). The following precautions can be taken to weaken the UTCA.

Firstly, give learners consistent reward or positive reinforcement for their speaking performance. According to the S—R learning theories (Brahmawong, 2006), positive reinforcement following responses can promote behavior. If an individual's attempt to communicate is repeatedly greeted with positive reinforcement/reward, he/she is less likely to feel anxious about communication. In other words, positive reinforcement/reward could bring down UTCA and consequently reduce SA. Secondly, provide learners sufficient chances for speaking, especially in formal, new or conspicuous situations, which are likely to cause higher apprehension of speaking. Practice serves two purposes, developing the speaking skill and helping learners to become desensitized to those situations, both of which are likely to reduce the UTCA and consequently lessen the SA.

(4) Help learners to improve their language achievement (LA). Poor learning is a source of language anxiety, because it is directly related to the high probability of failure in performance, which may further cause negative evaluations from others or oneself. Fear of negative evaluation is one of the three components of language anxiety suggested by Horwitz et al. (1991). Whatever approaches effective for improving language achievement are beneficial for reducing SA. Strategies such as strengthening the learners' motivation, increasing their self confidence, improving the efficiency of teaching and learning, taking good care of individual differences, etc., are all likely to improve the language achievement, and consequently reduce the SA. According

to the field theory (Brahmawong, 2006), language teachers can enhance learning by creating a need for the learners, engaging them in active learning, and involving them in appropriate environment.

(5) Help learners to modify their inappropriate beliefs, because beliefs are related to UTCA or SA. The modification of beliefs involves transformative or deep learning. The learners' existing assumptions and meaning schemes, if inappropriate or irrational, need to be criticized and challenged so as to bring about a reframing of their meaning perspective. Perfectionism (the unfeasibility of goals), and the rigid demands about perfectionism (irrational beliefs) are the two types of roots of psychological problems related to speaking performance. Rigid demands may lead to a series of other irrational beliefs and problems. To overcome those problems, language teachers can follow the concept framework of REBT and develop their own versions of speaking anxiety reduction techniques. Educationists can publish standardized models to save the work of language teachers.

7.4.3 Recommendations

This empirical study focused on the anxiety related to speaking performance. There could be anxiety related to other language skills, such as listening, reading, or writing, which is in need of exploration by future studies. Moreover, the language anxiety experienced by different populations, such as primary school learners, middle school learners, high school students, undergraduates, postgraduates, etc., may differ greatly. Future research with different populations could be expected to yield new findings about language anxiety. Except the variables tapped in the present study, language anxiety could be related to many other variables involved in the process of learning and teaching, which deserve the attention of researchers. For the specific remedies of language anxiety, the present study only tested the Psychoeducation lecture developed from the REBT. Other relevant techniques and psychotherapies are still in need of adaptation and empirical study.

7.5　Summary in Chinese

本章呈现了一项实证研究，着重考查了大学生的课堂口语焦虑水平、口语焦虑与其他相关变量的关系、心理教育讲座（见第六章）对于口语焦虑的影响等问题。研究对象为贵州财经学院的大学生，采用了调查（两次调查分别涉及 240 人和 103 人）和实验（涉及 32 人）相结合的研究方法。实验部分使用了一个干预组和一个控制组，干预组接受了前测（口语焦虑、口语状态焦虑和口语表达）、干预（接受有关心理教育讲座）和后测（同前测），控制组和干预组类似但没有接受干预部分。测量工具主要包括口语焦虑量表、特质焦虑量表、不愿交际倾向量表、语言课堂大胆尝试倾向量表、语言课堂互动倾向量表、口语自我效能感量表、口语状态焦虑量表等。数据采用 T 检验、卡方检验、结构方程建模、协方差分析等方法进行处理。研究结果显示：（1）学生的口语焦虑均值属于中等水平且无性别差异；（2）口语焦虑与特质焦虑和不愿交际倾向呈正相关，与语言成绩、口语自我效能感、语言课堂大胆尝试倾向和语言课堂互动倾向呈负相关；（3）口语焦虑可以通过不愿交际倾向（一个子成分）、语言课堂大胆尝试倾向和语言成绩进行回归预测；（4）口语焦虑和其他变量之间存在复杂的因果关系；（5）心理教育讲座干预能够降低口语焦虑和口语状态焦虑，并提高口语表达质量，其效果不受性别影响。

研究结果意味着，学生的口语焦虑应受到教育者的高度重视，因为焦虑影响着学生的口语表达和成绩。教师应采取不同策略，帮助学生克服语言焦虑，提高教学质量。

Chapter 8 Findings on emotion regulation strategies for language anxiety

Along with the development of globalization, foreign (or second) language teaching is becoming more and more important. Given the prevalence and negative effects of language anxiety, a lot of research has been devoted to the study of coping strategies. This chapter provides a brief review of studies on the effects of emotion regulation strategies, which are primarily psychotherapies transplanted to language learning settings.

Emotion regulation strategies can be put in two categories, relaxation techniques and cognitive behavioral therapies. Relaxation techniques include progressive muscle relaxation, autogenic training, guided imagery (visualization), mindfulness meditation and other contemplative practices, diaphragm breathing (deep/belly breathing), biofeedback, hypnosis (hypnotherapy), and so on. Cognitive and behavioral therapies refer to psychotherapies involving the modification of cognitions and/or behaviors. Systematic desensitization, cognitive restructuring and rational emotive behavioral therapy are simply typical examples.

8.1 Relaxation oriented emotion regulation strategies

(1) Mindfulness

Fallah (2017) investigated how language anxiety is related to mindfulness measured by Mindfulness Attention Awareness Scale (Brown & Ryan, 2003), finding that learners with lower levels of foreign language anxiety had higher levels of mindfulness. The result supports the effectiveness of mindfulness meditation as a technique for the alleviation of anxiety. Using a sample of Thai college students, Charoensukmongkol & Peerayuth (2016) examined whether mindfulness is related to ESL (English as a second language) speaking anxiety and presentation performance in the classrooms. Through partial least squares regression analysis, the researchers found that students with higher degrees of trait and state mindfulness during English speaking performance tended to have less anxiety in their presentations. The scores of presentations by students with low levels of anxiety were higher than those by students with high levels of anxiety. State mindfulness seemed to be capable of predicting ESL public speaking anxiety better than trait mindfulness. Charoensukmongkol & Peerayuth distinguished between state and trait mindfulness. Though both were related to speaking anxiety and performance, state mindfulness was found to be more closely associated with speaking anxiety.

Franco, et al. (2010) explored the influence of a mindfulness program on the levels of anxiety, academic performance, and self-concept among a group of secondary school students. The mindfulness program was given in a 1.5 hours' session every week for total of 10 weeks. During those sessions, the subjects learned and practiced a mindfulness technique called Meditación Fluir, and a body scan. For the Meditación Fluir exercise, the subjects were required to repeat a word or mantra, pay attention to the abdomen, imagine that they are breathing in and out of the abdomen, and focus on whatever thoughts emerging spontaneously in their mind. The thoughts were accepted as momentary mental events without reaction, judgment, evaluation or analysis. This was in fact a typical practice of mindfulness - based - cognitive therapy, which can raise awareness of currently ongoing experience. To reinforce the effect of the Meditación Fluir exercise, tales about the Zen tradition and Vipassana meditation, as well as various acceptance and commitment therapy metaphors and exercise were used, which could give emphasis to the belief that letting thoughts come and go freely is more constructive than trying to control them—controlling thoughts only results in more annoyance. The final results showed that the program was able to significantly increase academic performance, self-concept, and reduce anxiety states and traits.

(2) Combination of mindfulness with other contemplative practices

Contemplative practices (including mindfulness training), according to

Scida & Jones (2017), are techniques for quieting the mind, promoting a kind and compassionate attitude to oneself and others, and developing awareness of present experience with a receptive, nonjudgmental, and compassionate stance.

Scida & Jones (2017) explored the effects of a combination of contemplative practices on language anxiety, classroom climate, positive and negative affect, language learning, and self-efficacy among students in a university in America. The subjects were taught a variety of exercises including breath meditation, vision-setting, goal-setting, intention-setting, loving-kindness practice, rest the hands, body scan, just worrying labeling technique, mindful movement/stretching, visualization meditation, journaling and gratitude writing. The subjects were invited, but not required, to select their own favorite exercises to practice. The contemplative practice lasted for 5 to 10 minutes, and were performed at the beginning of a class approximately once per week. After a semester, the results showed that the practice had significant positive effects on classroom climate and achievement in language learning, but no significant effect on foreign language anxiety, affect or self-efficacy.

(3) Guided imagery

Önem (2015) explored the effect of guided imaginary (called meditation in the source paper) on anxiety and vocabulary learning among university students. Anxiety was measured by the State-Trait Anxiety scale. In each session of the experiment, the students practice a 10-minute meditation guided by a researcher before vocabulary learning. The students were required to close their eyes, breathe deeply and imagine peaceful events (e.g., to imagine staying on a sunny beach with the people they love, or going on a picnic in a park). To reinforce the effects, scent of lavender as well as an ordinary scent dispenser were employed in the classroom where the experiment took place. A two-week teaching and experimental study suggested that the meditation can significantly reduce anxiety and increase learning.

(4) Combination of guided imagery with progressive muscle relaxation

Arnold (2000) investigated the effects of guided imagery (visualization in the source work) and relaxation on listening test performance, listening self efficiency (termed beliefs about their abilities to understand spoken English), and attitude to listening test situations. The subjects used in the study were university students in Spain, who had difficulty in listening comprehension. The relaxation exercise involved focusing on the deep breathing, imagining breathing in harmony and breathing out tension, and progressively relaxing the whole body while breathing deeply.

The guided imagery trainings were performed in the state of relaxation in 6 sessions, with each given right before a practice test and lasting for 10 minutes. The exercises in the guided imaginary included (a) activating mental images in the first session, (b) learning to appreciate the brain and recognize that whatever stored in the brain was retrievable in the second session, (c) producing images on the right and the left sides of the brain, and imaging making friends with the brain in the third and fourth sessions, (d) visiting an imagined inner world in which a master teacher helped one grasp all the listening skills in the fifth session, (e) imagining that all the difficulties with English were put in a box which disappeared forever, and that they had another meeting with the mastery teacher, in the last session. The result showed that the combination of guided imagery and relaxation could improve the subjects' listening test performance, increase their listening self efficacy, and positively change their attitudes to listening tests (the subjects involved in the experiment felt more confident and relaxed after the treatment).

(5) Progressive muscle relaxation versus hypnosis

Dadashi et al. (2018) explored the effects of relaxation and hypnosis on EFL learners' test anxiety of female high school students. Each experimental session lasted 40 minutes, and was given twice a week during the two weeks of study. One group of subjects were given progressive muscle relaxation, and another were given hypnosis (positive suggestions given to subconscious mind for managing exam anxiety). It was found that both techniques could alleviate test anxiety, with hypnosis intervention producing a better effect than progressive muscle relaxation.

(6) Combination of biofeedback with diaphragm breathing, progressive muscle relaxation, and autogenic training

According to Somers & Jamieson (2014), at a University in Canada, Stress/Anxiety Management Education was offered to students in language classes. The education (self-regulation training) was labeled BMW. B was breathing (using cues of deep breathing, especially, diaphragm breathing, with exhalation longer than inhalation), M was muscles (using cues from muscle scanning and progressive muscle relaxation to alleviate tension in the waist, shoulders, neck, forehead, eyes, jaw), and W was WARM (using autogenic training techniques to increase blood circulation in the extremities). When students were familiar with them, BMW techniques could be completed in 15 sec to 3 minutes, and students were encouraged to frequently use them in a variety of daily situations, such as before a writing assignment, a presentation or an examination. To explore the influence of biofeedback on the Stress/Anxiety Management Education, some participants were provided HRV (heart rate variability) biofeedback as an additional technique (participants were given a cell-phone size portable biofeedback device, and they can observe their heart rate pattern shown in the form of a diagram on a small screen when their index fingers were inserted into a hole in the device). The results showed that biofeedback could help students better learn the regulation techniques. The researcher suggested that self-regulation training requires practice to produce noticeable effect, and the biofeedback can guide and motivate the practice.

(7) Combination of diaphragm breathing, meditation, and study coping skills

Vitasari et al. (2011) investigated the effect of diaphragm breathing, meditation (focusing on one thing to enter a state of calm, which is termed relaxation in the original work), and study coping skills (suggestions for successful learning, such as good habit of reviewing) on anxiety and language performance. Six university students majoring in engineering participated in the study, each of whom received six sessions of treatment, with each session lasting two hours. The results showed that the intervention could significantly reduce the participants' test anxiety measured by the number of breaths per-minute, though the GPA improvement was not significant.

8.2 Cognition and behavior oriented emotion regulation strategies

(1) Cognitive restructuring versus rational emotional behavioral therapy

Eifediyi (2015) investigated the effects of cognitive restructuring (called cognitive behavioral therapy in the source work) and rational emotive behavior therapy in coping with test anxiety among high school students. Two groups of subjects were sampled, with one group receiving the treatment of cognitive restructuring and the other receiving the treatment of rational emotive behavioral therapy. Both groups were treated for seven weeks. The results showed that both therapies could significantly reduce the subjects' test anxiety, with no significant difference in terms of effectiveness between the two types of therapies. In other words, the two techniques seemed equally effective for reducing the test anxiety of senior secondary school students.

(2) Combination of systematic desensitization, skills training, and cognitive restructuring

Docan-Morgan & Schmidt (2012) examined the effects of systematic desensitization, skills training, and cognitive restructuring on the public speaking anxiety of native and non-native speakers of English. All the participants were exposed to a one-hour session of public speaking anxiety training involving those techniques. The results showed that the treatment can reduce the public speaking anxiety of both the native and non-native speakers of English.

8.3 Summary in Chinese

随着全球化进程的加快，外语教学越来越重要。鉴于语言焦虑的普遍性及其消极影响，不少研究致力于考查应对焦虑的策略。如下是对情绪管理策略研究的一些案例概述。

第一，正念研究。不少调查或实验结果显示，正念能力越强，语言焦虑越低；正念冥想训练能够显著提高学习成绩和自我概念，降低语言焦虑水平。

第二，意象引导。针对意象引导与焦虑关系和与词汇学习关系的有关实验显示，意象引导能够降低焦虑，提高词汇学习成绩。

第三，渐进肌肉放松与催眠。有研究比较渐进肌肉放松与催眠对外语考试焦虑的影响，结果显示，两种方法都能显著降低考试焦虑，但催眠比渐进肌肉放松效果更强。

第四，理性情绪行为疗法。该法属于 CBT 范畴。有研究发现，理性情绪行为疗法训练能显著降低语言焦虑。

第五，综合研究。不少学者尝试将不同方法结合起来，对学生进行干预，检测其对语言焦虑的效果。研究一般获得了肯定性结果。

综观现有学术文献可知，情绪管理策略训练是应对语言焦虑的有效方法。

Bibliography

Aida, Y. , "Examination of Horwitz, Horwitz, and Cope's Construct of Foreign Language Anxiety: The Case of Students of Japanese", *Modern Language Journal*, 1994, 78 (2): 155-168.

Aihie, O. N. and Igbineweka, M. N. , "Efficacy of Solution Focused Brief Therapy, Systematic Desensitization and Rational Emotive Behavioural Therapy in Reducing the Test Anxiety Status of Undergraduates in a Nigerian University", *Journal of Educational and Social Research*, 2018, 8 (1): 19-26.

Albrecht, N. J. , "Teachers Teaching Mindfulness with Children: An Interpretative Phenomenological Analysis", doctoral dissertation, Flinders University, 2016.

Alpert, R. and Haber, R. N. , "Anxiety in Academic Achievement Situations", *Journal of Abnormal and Social Psychology*, 1960, 61 (2): 207-215.

Arnold, J. , "Seeing Through Listening Comprehension Exam Anxiety", *Tesol Quarterly*, 2000, 34 (4): 777-786.

Arnold, N. , "Reducing Foreign Language Communication Apprehension with Computer-Mediated Communication: A Preliminary Study", *System*, 2007, 35 (4): 469-486.

Ary, D. , Jacobs, L. C. , Razavieh, A. , and Sorensen, C. , *Introduction to Research in Education* (7th. Ed.), California: Thomson Wadsworth, 2006.

Bailey, K. M. , "Competitiveness and Anxiety in Adult Second Language Learning: Looking at and Through the Diary Studies", in Seliger, Herbert W. and Long, Michael H. (eds.), *Classroom Oriented Research*, Rowley: Newbury House, 1983.

Beck, A. T., "Thinking and Depression: Theory and Therapy", *Archives of General Psychiatry*, 1964, 10 (6): 561-571.

Beck, A. T., *Depression: Clinical, Experimental, and Theoretical*, New York: Hoeber, 1967.

Beck, A. T. and Emery, G., *Anxiety Disorders and Phobias: A Cognitive Perspective*, New York: Basic Books, 1985.

Bekleyen, N., "Foreign Language Anxiety", *Çukurova ÜNiversitesi Sosyal Bilimler EnstitÜSÜ Dergisi*, 2004, 13 (2): 24-40.

Benor, R., "Autogenic Training", *Complementary Therapies in Medicine*, 1996, 2 (5): 134-138.

Bluth, K., Campo, R. A., S., et al., "A School-Based Mindfulness Pilot Study for Ethnically Diverse at-Risk Adolescents", *Mindfulness*, 2016, 7 (1): 90-104.

Burgoon, J. K., "The Unwillingness-to-Communicate Scale: Development and Validation", *Communication Monographs*, 1976, 43 (1): 60-69.

Brahmawong, C., "VEBA: A Virtual Experience-Based Approach for Graduate Study in elearning", *Special Issue of the International Journal of the Computer: The Internet and Management*, 2006, 14 (10): 1-10.

Brown, J. S. L., Blackshaw, E., Stahl, D., et al., "School-Based Early Intervention for Anxiety and Depression in Older Adolescents: A Feasibility Randomised Controlled Trial of a Self-Referral Stress Management Workshop Programme (DISCOVER)", *Journal Of Adolescence*, 2019, 71: 150-161.

Brown, K. W. and Ryan, R. M., "The Benefits of Being Present: Mindfulness and Its Role in Psychological Well-Being", *Journal of Personality and Social Psychology*, 2003, 84 (4): 822-848.

Chan, Y. and Wu, G., "A Study of Foreign Language Anxiety of EFL Elementary School Students in Taipei County", *Journal of National Taipei Teachers College*, 2004, 17 (1): 287-320.

Chang, G. B. Y., "A Study of Anxiety in Chinese EFL Learners", *Teaching & Research*, 1996, 18: 67-90.

Charoensukmongkol P., "The Role of Mindfulness in Reducing English

Language Anxiety Among Thai College Students", *International Journal of Bilingual Education and Bilingualism*, 2019, 22 (4): 414-427.

Chastain, K., "Affective and Ability Factors in Second Language Acquisition", *Language Learning*, 1975, 25 (1): 153-161.

Chen, Q. and Liu, D., *Contemporary Educational Psychology*, Beijing: Beijing Normal University Press, 1997.

Cheng, Y., Horwitz, E. K., and Schallert, D. L., "Language Anxiety: Differentiating Writing and Speaking Components", *Language Learning*, 1999, 49 (3): 417-446.

Crookall, D. and Oxford, R., "Dealing with Anxiety: Some Practical Activities for Language Learners and Teacher Trainees", in Horwitz, Elaine K. and Young, Dolly J. (eds.), *Language Anxiety: From Theory and Research to Classroom Implications*, Englewood Cliffs: Prentice Hall, 1991.

Dadashi, M., Modirkhamaneh, S., and Dadashi, M., "Hypnosis vs. Progressive Muscle Relaxation as Cognitive - Therapeutic Interventions: Insights into Reducing EFL Learners' Test Anxiety", *International Journal of English Language & Translation Studies*, 2018, 6 (4): 69-77.

Dahbi, M., "Training EFL Students on Relaxation Techniques to Manage Test Taking Anxiety: An Action Research Project", *International Journal of English Language Teaching*, 2015, 2 (1): 61-67.

Daly, J., "Understanding Communication Apprehension: An Introduction for Language Educators", in Horwitz, Elaine K. and Young, Dolly J. (eds.), *Language Anxiety: From Theory and Research to Classroom Implications*, Englewood Cliffs: Prentice Hall, 1991.

Darwin, C. R., *The Expression of the Emotions in Man and Animals*, London: John Murray, 1872.

Djigunović, J. M., "Language Anxiety and Language Processing", *EUROSLA Yearbook*, 2006, 6 (1): 191-212.

Dobson, K. S., *Handbook of Cognitive-Behavioral Therapies*, New York: Guilford Press, 2010.

Docan-Morgan, T. and Schmidt, T., "Reducing Public Speaking Anxiety for Native and Non-Native English Speakers: The Value of Systematic

Desensitization, Cognitive Restructuring, and Skills Training", *Cross-Cultural Communication*, 2012, 8 (5): 16-19.

Donley, P. M., "The Foreign Language Anxieties and Anxiety Management Strategies of Students Taking Spanish at a Community College", doctoral dissertation, The University of Texas at Austin, 1997.

Dryden, W., *Reason to Change: A Rational Emotive Behaviour Therapy (REBT) Workbook*, Hove: Brunner/Routledge, 2001.

Elkhafaifi, H., "Listening Comprehension and Anxiety in the Arabic Language Classroom", *The Modern Language Journal*, 2005, 89 (2): 206-220.

Ellis, A., "Extending the Goals of Behavior Therapy and of Cognitive Behavior Therapy", *Behavior Therapy*, 1997, 28 (3): 333-339.

Ellis, A., *Rational Emotive Behavior Therapy: It Works for Me—It Can Work for You*, Amherst: Prometheus, 2004.

Ely, C. M., "An Analysis of Discomfort, Risk-Taking, Sociability, and Motivation in the L2 Classroom", *Language Learning*, 1986, 36 (1): 1-25.

Fallah, N., "Mindfulness, Coping Self-Efficacy and Foreign Language Anxiety: A Mediation Analysis", *Educational Psychology*, 2017, 37 (6): 745-756.

Felver, J. C., Celis-de Hoyos, C. E., Tezanos K, et al., "A Systematic Review of Mindfulness-Based Interventions for Youth in School Settings", *Mindfulness*, 2016, 7 (1): 34-45.

Felver, J. C. and Jennings, P. A., "Applications of Mindfulness-Based Interventions in School Settings: An Introduction", *Mindfulness*, 2016, 7 (1): 1-4.

Foss, K. A. and Reitzel, A. C., "A Relational Model for Managing Second Language Anxiety", in Horwitz, Elaine K. and Young, Dolly J. (eds.), *Language Anxiety: From Theory and Research to Classroom Implications*, Englewood Cliffs: Prentice Hall, 1991.

Franco, C., Mañas, I., Cangas, A. J., and Gallego, J., "The Applications of Mindfulness with Students of Secondary School: Results on the

Academic Performance, Self – Concept and Anxiety", World Summit on Knowledge Society, Berlin, 2010.

Frankfort-Nachmias, C. and Nachmias, D., *Research Methods in Social Science*, London: Arnold, 1996.

Galante, J., Dufour, G., Vainre, M., et al. "A Mindfulness-Based Intervention To Increase Resilience to Stress in University Students (The Mindful Student Study): A Pragmatic Randomised Controlled Trial", *The Lancet Public Health*, 2018, 3 (2): 72–81.

Gardner, H., *Frames of Mind: The Theory of Multiple Intelligences*, New York: Basik Books, 1983.

Gardner, R. C., Tremblay, P. F., and Masgoret, A., "Towards a Full Model of Second Language Learning: An Empirical Investigation", *Modern Language Journal*, 1997, 81 (3): 344–362.

Horwitz, E. K., "Language Anxiety and Achievement", *Annual Review of Applied Linguistics*, 2001, 21: 112–126.

Horwitz, E. K., Horwitz, M. B., and Cope, J. A., "Foreign Language Classroom Anxiety", *Modern Language Journal*, 1986, 70 (2): 125–132.

Horwitz E., "Preliminary Evidence for the Reliability and Validity of a Foreign Language Anxiety Scale", in Horwitz, Elaine K. and Young, Dolly J. (eds.), *Language Anxiety: From Theory and Research to Classroom Implications*, Englewood Cliffs: Prentice Hall, 1991.

Horwitz, E. K., Horwitz, M. B., and Cope J. A., "Foreign Language Classroom Anxiety", *Language Anxiety: From Theory and Research to Classroom Implications*, Ed. Elaine K. Horwitz, Dolly J. Young, Englewood Cliffs: Prentice Hall, 1991: 27–36.

Hou, Y., "The Causes of Communication Apprehension and the Ways to Tackle Them", *Journal of Baoding Teacher's College*, 2004, 17 (1): 106–108.

Ifeanyi, I., Nwokolo, C., and Anyamene, A., "Effects of Systematic Desensitisation Technique on Test Anxiety among Secondary School Students", *International Journal of Humanities Social Sciences and Education (IJHSSE)*, 2015, 2 (2): 167–178.

Ikonić, D. and Hawes, T. , "The Influence of Autogenic Training on Listening Comprehension in the English Classroom", *Linguistics Journal*, 2017, 7: 32-35.

Jacobson, E. , *Progressive Muscle Relaxation*, Chicago: University of Chicago Press, 1938.

Jacobson, E. , *Progressive Muscle Relaxation: How to Reduce the Physical Feeling of Induced Worries (Anxiety) by Using Relaxation*? (https://Is. Muni. Cz/El/1421/Podzim2016/PSX_ 111/Um/Jacobson_ Progressive_ Muscle_ Relaxation_ Eng. Pdf).

James, W. , "What Is An Emotion?", *Mind*, 1884, 9 (34): 188-205.

Jones, S. M. , "The Influence of Native Language on the Treatment of Language Anxiety among an English-as-a-Second-Language-Speaking Population", doctoral dissertation, The University of Wisconsin-Milwaukee, 2002.

Kassel, S. C. , "Stress Management and Peak Performance Crash Course for Ninth Graders in a Charter School Setting", *Biofeedback*, 2015, 43 (2): 90-93.

Kitano, K. , "Anxiety in the College Japanese Language Classroom", *Modern Language Journal*, 2001, 85 (4): 549-566.

Krashen, S. D. , *Principles and Practice in Second Language Acquisition*, New York: Pergamon, 1982.

Kwee, M. , "Wherever You Go, There You Are: Mindfulness Meditation in Everyday Life", *Behaviour Research and Therapy*, 1995, 33 (8): 996.

Leary, M. R. , "Social Anxiety", in Wheeler, Ladd (ed.), *Review of Personality And Social Psychology*, Beverly Hills: Sage, 1982.

Liu, M. , "Anxiety in Chinese EFL Students at Different Proficiency Levels", *System*, 2006, 34 (3): 301-316.

Liu, M. and Jackson, J. , "An Exploration of Chinese EFL Learners' Unwillingness to Communicate and Foreign Language Anxiety", *The Modern Language Journal*, 2008, 92 (1): 71-86.

López-González, L. , Amutio, A. , Oriol X. , et al. , "Habits Related to Relaxation and Mindfulness of High School Students: Influence on Classroom Climate and Academic Performance", *Revista de Psicodidáctica*, 2016, 21 (1): 121-138.

Machida, S., "Test Anxiety in Japanese-Language Class Oral Examinations", *Sekai No Nihongo Kyoiku*, 2001, 11: 115-138.

Macintyre, P. D., "How Does Anxiety Affect Second Language Learning? A Reply to Sparks and Ganshow", *The Modern Language Journal*, 1995, 79 (1): 90-99.

Macintyre, P. D., "Language Anxiety: A Review of the Research for Language Teachers", in Young, Dolly J. (ed.), *Affect in Foreign Language and Second Language Learning: A Practical Guide to Creating a Low-Anxiety Classroom Atmosphere*, Boston: Mcgraw-Hill, 1999.

Macintyre, P. D., Baker S. C., ClÉMent, R., and Donovan, L. A., "Sex and Age Effects on Willingness to Communicate, Anxiety, Perceived Competence, and L2 Motivation among Junior High School French Immersion Students", *Language Learning*, 2002, 52 (3): 537-564.

Macintyre, P. D. and Gardner, R. C., "Anxiety and Second Language Learning: Toward a Theoretical Clarification", in Horwitz, Elaine K. and Young, Dolly J. (eds.), *Language Anxiety: From Theory and Research to Classroom Implications*, Englewood Cliffs: Prentice Hall, 1991a.

Macintyre, P. D. and Gardner, R. C., "Language Anxiety: Its Relation to Other Anxieties and to Processing in Native and Second Languages", *Language Learning*, 1991b, 41 (4): 513-534.

Macintyre, P. D. and Gardner, R. C., "Methods and Results in the Study of Anxiety in Language Learning: A Review of the Literature", *Language Learning*, 1991c, 41 (1): 85-117.

Macintyre, P. D. and Gardner, R. C., "The Effects of Induced Anxiety on Three Stages of Cognitive Processing in Computerized Vocabulary Learning", *Studies in Second Language Acquisition*, 1994a, 16 (1): 1-17.

Macintyre, P. D. and Gardner, R. C., "The Subtle Effects of Language Anxiety on Cognitive Processing in the Second Language", *Language Learning*, 1994b, 44 (2): 283-305.

Macintyre, P. D., Noels K. A., and ClÉMent, R., "Biases in Self-Ratings of Second Language Proficiency: The Role of Language Anxiety", *Language Learning*, 1997, 47 (2): 265-287.

Madsen, H. S., Brown, B. L., and Jones, R. L., "Evaluating Student Attitudes Toward Second-Language Tests", in Horwitz, Elaine K. and Young, Dolly J. (eds.), *Language Anxiety: From Theory and Research to Classroom Implications*, Englewood Cliffs: Prentice Hall, 1991.

Matsuda, S. and Gobel, P., "Anxiety and Predictors of Performance in the Foreign Language Classroom", *System*, 2004, 32 (1): 21-36.

May. R., *The Meaning of Anxiety*, New York: Washington Square Press, 1977.

Mcgrath, T., Tsui, E., Humphries, S., and Yule, W., "Successful Treatment of a Noise Phobia in a Nine-Year-Old Girl with Systematic Desensitization in Vivo", *Educational Psychology*, 1990, 10 (1): 79-83.

Mejías, H., Applebaum, R. L., Applebaum S. J., and Trotter, R. T., "Oral Communication Apprehension and Hispanics: An Exploration of Oral Communication Apprehension among Mexican American Students in Texas", in Horwitz, Elaine K. and Young, Dolly J. (eds.), *Language Anxiety: From Theory and Research to Classroom Implications*, Englewood Cliffs: Prentice Hall, 1991.

Mercer, S., "Learner self-beliefs", *ELT Journal*, 2008, 62 (2): 182-183.

Mertens, D. M., *Research Methods in Education and Psychology: Integrating Diversity with Qualitative and Quantitative Approaches*, California: Sage Publications, 1998.

Mezirow, J., *Education for Perspective Transformation: Women's Re-Entry Programs in Community Colleges*, New York: Columbia University, 1975.

Mezirow, J., *Transformative Dimensions of Adult Learning*, San Francisco: Jossey-Bass, 1991.

Mezirow, J., "Learning to Think Like an Adult: Core Concepts of Transformation Theory", in Jack Mezirow (ed.), *Learning as Transformation*,

San Francisco: Jossey-Bass, 2000.

Nei, J., *Reason to Change: A Rational Emotive Behavioral Therapy*, Beijing: China Light Industry Press, 2009.

Nurhuda, F., Hidayah, T. H. T., and Soenyoto, T., "The Influence of Mental Imagery and Psychological Relaxation toward Confidence and Anxiety on Pre Junior Rhythmic Athletes", *Journal of Physical Education and Sports*, 2019, 8 (3): 237-245.

Ohata, K., "Potential Sources of Anxiety for Japanese Learners of English: Preliminary Case Interviews with Five Japanese College Students in the U.S", *TESL-EJ*, 2005, 9 (3): 1-21.

Önem, E. E., "A Study on the Effects of Meditation on Anxiety and Foreign Language Vocabulary Learning", *Journal of Language and Literature Education*, 2015, 15: 134-148.

Onwuegbuzie, A. J., Bailey, P., and Daley, C. E., "Cognitive, Affective, Personality, and Demographic Predictors of Foreign Language Achievement", *Journal of Educational Research*, 2001, 94 (1): 3-15.

Orne, M. T., "The Nature of Hypnosis: Artifact and Essence", *Journal of Abnormal Psychology*, 1959, 58 (3): 277-299.

Otta, F. E. and Ogazie, C. A., "Effects of Systematic Desensitization and Study Behaviour Techniques on the Reduction of Test Phobia among in-School Adolescents in Abia State", *World*, 2014, 1 (3): 1-7.

Oxford, R. L., *Language Learning Strategies: What Every Teacher Should Know*, Boston: Heinle & Heinle, 1990.

Panneerselvam, S. and Govindharaj, P., "Effectiveness of Guided Imagery in Reducing Examination Anxiety among Secondary School Students in South India", *The International Journal of Indian Psychology*, 2016, 3 (3): 54-61.

Peng, D., *General Psychology*, Beijing: Beiing Normal University Press, 2001.

Phillips, E. M., "The Effects of Language Anxiety on Students' Oral Test Performance and Attitudes", *The Modern Language Journal*, 1992, 76 (1): 14-26.

Price, M. L., "The Subjective Experiences of Foreign Language Anxiety: Interviews with Anxious Students", in Horwitz, Flaine K. and Young, Dolly J. (eds.), *Language Anxiety: From Theory and Research to Classroom Implications*, Englewood Cliffs: Prentice Hall, 1991: 101–108.

Qureshi, M., "The Views of Young People about an Intervention Programme Designed To Support Them with Exam Related Anxiety and Stress", doctoral dissertation, University of East London, 2016.

Raes, F., Griffith, J. W., Van der Gucht, K., et al., "School - Based Prevention and Reduction of Depression in Adolescents: A Cluster - Randomized Controlled Trial of a Mindfulness Group Program", *Mindfulness*, 2014, 5 (5): 477–486.

Rajiah, K. and Saravanan, C., "The Effectiveness of Psychoeducation and Systematic Desensitization to Reduce Test Anxiety among First - Year Pharmacy Students", *American Journal of Pharmaceutical Education*, 2014, 78 (9): 1–7.

Rasid, Z. and Parish, T. S., "The Effects of Two Types of Relaxation Training on Students' Levels of Anxiety", *Adolescence*, 1998, 33 (129): 99–101.

Scida, E. E. and Jones, J. N., "The Impact of Contemplative Practices on Foreign Language Anxiety and Learning", *Studies in Second Language Learning and Teaching*, 2017, 7 (4): 573–599.

Schonert - Reichl, K. A., Oberle, E., Lawlor, M. S., et al., "Enhancing Cognitive and Social-Emotional Development Through a Simple-To - Administer Mindfulness - Based School Program for Elementary School Children: A Randomized Controlled Trial", *Developmental Psychology*, 2015, 51 (1): 52–66.

Schultz, J. H., *Das Autogene Training—Konzentrative Selbstentspannung*, Leipzig: Thieme, 1932.

Schwartz, M. S. and Andrasik, F., *Biofeedback: A Practitioner's Guide*, New York: Guilford Publications, 2017.

Schwarz, R. L., *Learning Disabilities and Foreign Language Learning*, 1997 (www. Ldonline. Org/Article/6065).

Scovel, T., "The Effect of Affect on Foreign Language Learning: A Review of the Anxiety Research", *Language Learning*, 1978, 28 (1): 129-142.

Segal, Z., Teasdale, J., and Williams, M., *Mindfulness - Based Cognitive Therapy for Depression*, New York: Guilford Press, 2002.

Sharma, M., "Secondary School Students - Systematic Desensitisation Technique on Test Anxiety", *International Journal of Innovative Studies in Sociology and Humanities*, 2018, 3 (3): 27-34.

Snyder, C. R., and Ray, W. J., "Observed Body Movement in the College Test-Taking Situation and the Scholastic Aptitude Test", *Perceptual and Motor Skills*, 1971, 32 (1): 265-266.

Somers, K. and Jamieson, S., "Stress and Anxiety in (Second Language) Learning: Using HRV Biofeedback and Stress Management Education to Facilitate Learning Success", *TESL Ontario CONTACT Magazine*, 2014, 40 (1): 29-35.

Sparks, R. L. and Ganschow, L., "Foreign Language Learning Differences: Affective or Native Language Aptitude Differences?", *Modern Language Journal*, 1991, 75 (1): 3-16.

Sparks, R. L. and Ganschow, L. "The Impact of Native Language Learning Problems on Foreign Language Learning: Illustrations of the Linguistic Coding Deficit Hypothesis", *Modern Language Journal*, 1993a, 77 (1): 58-74.

Sparks, R. and Ganschow, L., "Searching for the Cognitive Locus of Foreign Language Learning Difficulties: Linking First and Second Language Learning", *Modern Language Journal*, 1993b, 77 (3): 289-302.

Sparks, R. L. and Ganschow, L., "Is the Foreign Language Classroom Anxiety Scale Measuring Anxiety or Language Skills?", *Foreign Language Annals*, 2007, 40 (2): 260-287.

Spielberger, C. D., "The Nature and Measurement of Anxiety", in Spielberger, Charles. D., Diaz-Guerrero, Rogelio (eds.), *Cross-Cultural Anxiety*, Washington: Hemisphere Publishing Corporation, 1976.

Spielberger, C. D., *Manual for the State-Trait Anxiety Inventory (STAI-*

Form Y), Palo Alto: Consulting Psychologists Press, 1983.

Steinberg, F. S. and Horwitz, E. K., "The Effect of Induced Anxiety on the Denotative and Interpretive Content of Second Language Speech", *TESOL Quarterly*, 1986, 20 (1): 131-136.

Swain, M. and Burnaby, B., "Personality Characteristics and Second Language Learning in Young Children: A Pilot Study", *Working Papers in Bilingualism*, 1976, 11: 115-128.

Tiono, N. I. and Sylvia, A., "The Types of Communication Strategies Used by Speaking Class Students with Different Communication Apprehension Levels in English Department of Petra Christian University, Surabaya", doctoral dissertation, Petra Christian University, 2004.

Tucker, R., Hamayan, E., and Genesee, F. H., "Affective, Cognitive, and Social Factors in Second Language Acquisition", *Canadian Modern Language Review*, 1976, 32 (3): 214-226.

Tusek, D. L., Church, J. M., Strong, S. A., Grass, J. A., and Fazio, V. W., "Guided Imagery", *Diseases of the Colon & Rectum*, 1997, 40 (2): 172-178.

Valentine, K. E., Milling, L. S., Clark, L. J., et al., "The Efficacy of Hypnosis as a Treatment for Anxiety: A Meta-analysis", *International Journal of Clinical and Experimental Hypnosis*, 2019, 67 (3): 336-363.

Van De Weijer-Bergsma E., Langenberg G., Brandsma R., et al., "The Effectiveness of a School-Based Mindfulness Training as a Program to Prevent Stress in Elementary School Children", *Mindfulness*, 2014, 5 (3): 238-248.

Veena, D. and Alvi, S., "Guided Imagery Intervention for Anxiety Reduction", *Indian Journal of Health and Wellbeing*, 2016, 7 (2): 198-203.

Vitasari, P., Wahab, M. N. A., Herawan, T., Othman, A., and Sinnadurai, S. K., "A Pilot Study of Pre-Post Anxiety Treatment to Improve Academic Performance for Engineering Students", *Procedia - Social and Behavioral Sciences*, 2011, 15: 3826-3830.

Wei, M., "The Interrelatedness of Affective Factors in EFL Learning:

An Examination of Motivational Patterns in Relation to Anxiety in China", *TESL-EJ*, 2007, 11 (1): 1–23.

Weinrach, S. G., "Rational Emotive Behavior Therapy: A Tough-Minded Therapy for a Tender-Minded Profession", *Journal of Counseling and Development*, 1995, 73 (3): 296–300.

Wilson, J. S., *Anxiety in Learning English as a Foreign Language: Its Associations with Student Variables, with Overall Proficiency, and with Performance on an Oral Test*, 2006 (http://hera.ugr.es/tesisugr/16235290.pdf).

Wolpe, J., *Psychotherapy by Reciprocal Inhibition*, Stanford: Stanford University Press, 1958.

Woodrow, L. J., "Anxiety and Speaking English as a Second Language", *Regional Language Centre Journal*, 2006, 37 (3): 308–328.

Wright, J. H., "Cognitive Behavior Therapy: Basic Principles and Recent Advances", *Focus*, 2006, 4 (2): 173–178.

Xing, J., "Language Anxiety and Corresponding Strategies in College English Class", *Journal of Lishui University*, 2007, 29 (6): 118–120.

Young, D. J., "The Relationship between Anxiety and Foreign Language Oral Proficiency Ratings", *Foreign Language Annals*, 1986, 19 (5): 439–445.

Young, D. J., "Creating a Low-Anxiety Classroom Environment: What Does the Language Anxiety Research Suggest?", *Modern Language Journal*, 1991, 75 (4): 426–437.

Zhang, X., Yang, L., Liang, B., Wang, Z., and Shao X., "Self-Esteem as a Mediator of the Link between Perfectionism and Depression", *Studies of Psychology and Behavior*, 2008, 6 (3): 217–222.

Zhang, Y. Y., "On the Application of Cognitive Behavioral Therapy in Treating Foreign Language Listening Anxiety", *Studies in Literature and Language*, 2017, 15 (2): 26–31.

Zheng, Y., "Anxiety and Second/Foreign Language Learning Revisited", *Canadian Journal for New Scholars in Education*, 2008, 1 (1): 1–12.

Appendixes

Appendix A　Speaking Anxiety Scale
口语焦虑量表

（仅供研究，请如实填写各项，包括姓名）

姓名_____　性别（男，女）　年龄_____

指导语：下面列出的是一些英语学习者常常用来描述自己的句子，请阅读每一个句子，根据自己通常的感觉进行选择。回答没有优劣或对错之分，关键是符合实际。对每一陈述，无需反复思考，请凭第一印象作答。每个题都要做出选择（画勾"√"）。

1. 英语课上说英语时，我从来没有信心十足的感觉。

（A）完全同意　（B）同意　（C）不确定　（D）不同意　（E）完全不同意

2. 英语课上，当我知道自己要被老师提问时感到发抖。

（A）完全同意　（B）同意　（C）不确定　（D）不同意　（E）完全不同意

3. 我不担忧英语课上犯错误。

（A）完全同意　（B）同意　（C）不确定　（D）不同意　（E）完全不同意

4. 英语课上，在毫无准备的情况下需要说英语时，我开始感到惊慌。

（A）完全同意　（B）同意　（C）不确定　（D）不同意　（E）完全不同意

5. 英语课上，主动举手发言我觉得不好意思。

（A）完全同意　（B）同意　（C）不确定　（D）不同意　（E）完全不同意

6. 我在英语课上说英语时,感到自信。

(A) 完全同意　(B) 同意　(C) 不确定　(D) 不同意
(E) 完全不同意

7. 英语课上,当我自己要被老师提问时,我感到心在怦怦直跳。

(A) 完全同意　(B) 同意　(C) 不确定　(D) 不同意
(E) 完全不同意

8. 我总是觉得其他同学英语说得比我好。

(A) 完全同意　(B) 同意　(C) 不确定　(D) 不同意
(E) 完全不同意

9. 在班上说英语时,我感觉很轻松。

(A) 完全同意　(B) 同意　(C) 不确定　(D) 不同意
(E) 完全不同意

10. 说英语要遵循那么多规则,真是压倒人。

(A) 完全同意　(B) 同意　(C) 不确定　(D) 不同意
(E) 完全不同意

11. 在其他同学面前说英语,我觉得害羞、不自然。

(A) 完全同意　(B) 同意　(C) 不确定　(D) 不同意
(E) 完全不同意

12. 在毫无准备情况下被英语老师提问,我感到自然、放松。

(A) 完全同意　(B) 同意　(C) 不确定　(D) 不同意
(E) 完全不同意

13. 说英语时,我总害怕别的同学嘲笑我。

(A) 完全同意　(B) 同意　(C) 不确定　(D) 不同意
(E) 完全不同意

14. 我担心老师时刻都会纠正我的各种口语错误。

(A) 完全同意　(B) 同意　(C) 不确定　(D) 不同意
(E) 完全不同意

15. 与英语为母语的人交谈时,我不会感到紧张。

(A) 完全同意　(B) 同意　(C) 不确定　(D) 不同意
(E) 完全不同意

Appendix B Questionnaire on Disposition and Learning
心理与学习调查问卷

（请如实填写各项，包括姓名）

姓名_____ 性别（男，女） 年龄_____

指导语：下面列出的是一些同学们常常用来描述自己的句子，请阅读每一个句子，然后根据自己通常的感觉进行选择。回答没有对、错、优、劣之分，不要对任何一个句子花太多的时间去考虑，但做出的选择，应最符合你通常的感觉。注意每个题都要做出选择（画勾"√"）。

第一部分 普通心理（General Disposition）

（一）特质焦虑量表（Trait Anxiety Scale）

1. 我通常感到愉快。　　　　　　（没有，有点，中度，非常）
2. 我通常感到自我满意。　　　　（没有，有点，中度，非常）
3. 我感到精力充沛。　　　　　　（没有，有点，中度，非常）
4. 我通常是冷静、镇定和泰然的。（没有，有点，中度，非常）
5. 我通常是高兴的。　　　　　　（没有，有点，中度，非常）
6. 我缺乏自信心。　　　　　　　（没有，有点，中度，非常）
7. 我感到安全。　　　　　　　　（没有，有点，中度，非常）
8. 我容易做出决断。　　　　　　（没有，有点，中度，非常）
9. 我通常感到心满意足。　　　　（没有，有点，中度，非常）
10. 我是一个稳重的人。　　　　　（没有，有点，中度，非常）

（二）不愿沟通量表（Unwillingness to Communicate Scale）

1. 在交谈中，我不敢畅所欲言。

　　（A）完全同意　（B）同意　（C）不确定　（D）不同意（E）完全不同意

2. 我不爱说话，因为我害羞。

　　（A）完全同意　（B）同意　（C）不确定　（D）不同意（E）完全不同意

3. 我爱说话，因为我不害羞。

　　（A）完全同意　（B）同意　（C）不确定　（D）不同意

（E）完全不同意

4. 我喜欢卷入集体讨论。

（A）完全同意　（B）同意　（C）不确定　（D）不同意（E）完全不同意

5. 当我需要和别人说话时，我感到紧张。

（A）完全同意　（B）同意　（C）不确定　（D）不同意（E）完全不同意

6. 在群体中表达个人观点，我不害怕。

（A）完全同意　（B）同意　（C）不确定　（D）不同意（E）完全不同意

7. 在群体中表达个人观点，我感到害怕。

（A）完全同意　（B）同意　（C）不确定　（D）不同意（E）完全不同意

8. 我回避群体讨论。

（A）完全同意　（B）同意　（C）不确定　（D）不同意（E）完全不同意

9. 在会话过程中，我喜欢说，而不是喜欢听。

（A）完全同意　（B）同意　（C）不确定　（D）不同意（E）完全不同意

10. 和陌生人讲话，我觉得轻松。

（A）完全同意　（B）同意　（C）不确定　（D）不同意（E）完全不同意

11. 在和我沟通时，我认为我的朋友缺乏真诚性。

（A）完全同意　（B）同意　（C）不确定　（D）不同意（E）完全不同意

12. 我的朋友和家人不听我的主意和建议。

（A）完全同意　（B）同意　（C）不确定　（D）不同意（E）完全不同意

13. 我认为我的朋友对我真诚。

（A）完全同意　（B）同意　（C）不确定　（D）不同意（E）完全不同意

14. 需要做出决定时，我不向家人或朋友征求意见。

（A）完全同意　（B）同意　（C）不确定　（D）不同意（E）完全不同意

15. 我相信，我的家人和朋友理解我的情感。

（A）完全同意　（B）同意　（C）不确定　（D）不同意（E）完全不同意

16. 我的家人不喜欢和我一起讨论我的兴趣和活动。

（A）完全同意　（B）同意　（C）不确定　（D）不同意（E）完全不同意

17. 我的朋友和家人能够听进我的主意和建议。

（A）完全同意　（B）同意　（C）不确定　（D）不同意（E）完全不同意

18. 我的朋友征求我的意见和建议。

（A）完全同意　（B）同意　（C）不确定　（D）不同意（E）完全不同意

19. 别人对我友好，只是因为他们想从我这里得到什么。

（A）完全同意　（B）同意　（C）不确定　（D）不同意（E）完全不同意

20. 和别人谈话浪费时间，没有什么意义。

（A）完全同意　（B）同意　（C）不确定　（D）不同意（E）完全不同意

第二部分　英语学习心理（English Learning Disposition）

（一）口语焦虑量表（Speaking Anxiety Scale）

1. 英语课上说英语时，我从来没有信心十足的感觉。

（A）完全同意　（B）同意　（C）不确定　（D）不同意（E）完全不同意

2. 英语课上，当我知道自己要被老师提问时感到发抖。

（A）完全同意　（B）同意　（C）不确定　（D）不同意（E）完全不同意

3. 我不担忧英语课上犯错误。

（A）完全同意　（B）同意　（C）不确定　（D）不同意（E）完全不同意

4. 英语课上，在毫无准备的情况下需要说英语时，我开始感到惊慌。
（A）完全同意　（B）同意　（C）不确定　（D）不同意
（E）完全不同意

5. 英语课上，主动举手发言我觉得不好意思。
（A）完全同意　（B）同意　（C）不确定　（D）不同意
（E）完全不同意

6. 我在英语课上说英语时，感到自信。
（A）完全同意　（B）同意　（C）不确定　（D）不同意
（E）完全不同意

7. 英语课上，当我自己要被老师提问时，我感到心在怦怦直跳。
（A）完全同意　（B）同意　（C）不确定　（D）不同意
（E）完全不同意

8. 我总是觉得其他同学英语说得比我好。
（A）完全同意　（B）同意　（C）不确定　（D）不同意
（E）完全不同意

9. 在班上说英语时，我感觉很轻松。
（A）完全同意　（B）同意　（C）不确定　（D）不同意
（E）完全不同意

10. 说英语要遵循那么多规则，真是压倒人。
（A）完全同意　（B）同意　（C）不确定　（D）不同意
（E）完全不同意

11. 在其他同学面前说英语，我觉得害羞、不自然。
（A）完全同意　（B）同意　（C）不确定　（D）不同意
（E）完全不同意

12. 在毫无准备情况下被英语老师提问，我感到自然、放松。
（A）完全同意　（B）同意　（C）不确定　（D）不同意
（E）完全不同意

13. 说英语时，我总害怕别的同学嘲笑我。
（A）完全同意　（B）同意　（C）不确定　（D）不同意
（E）完全不同意

14. 我担心老师时刻都会纠正我的各种口语错误。
（A）完全同意　（B）同意　（C）不确定　（D）不同意

（E）完全不同意

15. 与英语为母语的人交谈时，我不会感到紧张。

（A）完全同意　　（B）同意　　（C）不确定　　（D）不同意
（E）完全不同意

（二）语言课堂尝试倾向（1-6）与社交倾向（7-11）量表 (Language Class Risk-Taking & Sociability Scales)

1. 我喜欢等到自己知道一个单词的精确用法时，才开始用它。

（A）完全同意　　（B）同意　　（C）不确定　　（D）不同意
（E）完全不同意

2. 我不喜欢在课堂上尝试使用较难的英语句子。

（A）完全同意　　（B）同意　　（C）不确定　　（D）不同意
（E）完全不同意

3. 目前，我不喜欢在课堂上试图用英语表达复杂的思想。

（A）完全同意　　（B）同意　　（C）不确定　　（D）不同意
（E）完全不同意

4. 我倾向于用英语表达自己想说的东西，而不担忧语法细节。

（A）完全同意　　（B）同意　　（C）不确定　　（D）不同意
（E）完全不同意

5. 英语课上，开口说一个句子之前，我倾向于自我默念一边。

（A）完全同意　　（B）同意　　（C）不确定　　（D）不同意
（E）完全不同意

6. 我倾向于模仿使用基本的句子结构模式，而不喜欢去冒错用之险。

（A）完全同意　　（B）同意　　（C）不确定　　（D）不同意
（E）完全不同意。

7. 我认为在集体中学英语比单独自学更有乐趣。

（A）完全同意　　（B）同意　　（C）不确定　　（D）不同意
（E）完全不同意

8. 我喜欢用英语和老师及同学交谈。

（A）完全同意　　（B）同意　　（C）不确定　　（D）不同意
（E）完全不同意

9. 在英语课上，我喜欢和其他同学交流。

（A）完全同意　　（B）同意　　（C）不确定　　（D）不同意

(E）完全不同意

10. 我认为，在英语课堂中，一种强烈的集体精神非常重要。

（A）完全同意　（B）同意　（C）不确定　（D）不同意
（E）完全不同意

11. 我希望课堂活动丰富一点，以便同学们使用英语更好地相互了解。

（A）完全同意　（B）同意　（C）不确定　（D）不同意
（E）完全不同意

12. 我的高考英语成绩是＿＿＿分。

第三部分　英语口语技能等级自评量表
（Speaking Self-Efficacy Scale）

陈　　述	自评级别（√）
1. 我能用英语回答课堂提问，能用通俗词汇和句型与同学进行主题式讨论。	1，2，3，4，5
2. 我能用英语介绍自己、同学、朋友等，并能对他人的介绍做出回应。	1，2，3，4，5
3. 我能用简单英语及手势为人指路、购物、留言、提出申请等。	1，2，3，4，5
4. 我能用英语数字报告时间、询问价格、回答电话号码等。	1，2，3，4，5
5. 我能与英语国家人士就日常话题进行简单交谈。	1，2，3，4，5
6. 我掌握了基本英语会话策略，如开始、继续或结束会话，让人重复所说内容或放慢语速等等。	1，2，3，4，5
7. 我的英语口语技能综合水平自评等级。	1，2，3，4，5

注："1"表示最低自评级别，"5"表示最高自评级别。

Appendix C　Speaking State Anxiety Scale
口语状态焦虑量表

（仅供研究，请如实填写各项，包括姓名）

姓名_____　　高考英语成绩____　（成绩填写仅在量表后测时要求）

指导语：如下句子试图描述你现在的感觉。请根据真实情况进行选择。回答没有优劣或对错之分，关键是符合实际。对每一陈述，无需反复思考，请凭第一印象作答。每个题都要做出选择（画勾"√"）。

1. 我担心会想不起来需要的词语。

（A）完全同意　（B）同意　（C）不确定　（D）不同意　（E）完全不同意

2. 我担心会说出错误的句子。

（A）完全同意　（B）同意　（C）不确定　（D）不同意　（E）完全不同意

3. 我担心自己的发音会引人发笑。

（A）完全同意　（B）同意　（C）不确定　（D）不同意　（E）完全不同意

4. 我担心会用错冠词。

（A）完全同意　（B）同意　（C）不确定　（D）不同意　（E）完全不同意

5. 我担心表达中断，说不下去。

（A）完全同意　（B）同意　（C）不确定　（D）不同意　（E）完全不同意

6. 我担心犯语法错误。

（A）完全同意　（B）同意　（C）不确定　（D）不同意　（E）完全不同意

7. 我担心发音出错。

（A）完全同意　（B）同意　（C）不确定　（D）不同意　（E）完全不同意

8. 我担心表达不够流利。

（A）完全同意　（B）同意　（C）不确定　（D）不同意　（E）完全不同意

Appendix D Speaking Performance Assessment Criteria
口语评定标准

1. The criteria

The speaking performance is judged by:

(1) The number of total words in all the Communication Units (CUs);

(2) The percent of words in mazes: number of words in mazes / (number of words in mazes + number of words in CUs) × 100%;

(3) The number of dependent clauses.

2. Definitions and Explanations of key Terms

(1) Communication Unites (CU)

They are independent clauses in English with all their modifiers, which may be correct or incorrect.

    a. A CU must be a unit of comprehensible speech.

    b. A simple sentence is a CU.

    e. g. I have a pen.　　(1 CU)

    c. A complex sentence is a CU.

    e. g. I have a pen which was given to me by my friend. (1 CU)

    d. A compound sentence includes 2 or more CUs, according to the number of independent clauses joined by coordinators, and the coordinators belong to the succeeding clauses.

    e. g. I have a pen, but I have no pencil. (2 CUs)

    e. An incomplete sentence (word, or phrase) that attempts to express a complete thought is also a CU.

    e. g. About ten o'clock. (1 CU)

(2) Mazes

A maze refers to everything that does not belong to a CU. A maze is a series of words (or initial parts of words), or unattached fragments which do not constitute a CU and are not necessary to a CU.

    a. Stuttering and repetitions are mazes.

    e. g. *The teacher the teacher is is very nice* is very nice. (2 mazes)

b. Message abandonment belongs to a maze.

e. g. Don't worry about me. *And don't worry*… (1 maze)

c. Words in L1 not essential to a CU belong to a maze.

e. g The SHU is very interesting. (0 maze: SHU (book) is a Chinese word but essential to the CU, so it is not a maze.)

(3) Dependent Clauses

Clauses which can not stand alone.

3. Rating Procedure

(1) Transcribe the speech recording verbatim.

(2) Check the transcription and improve it when it is necessary.

(3) Ask a peer researcher to check the transcription and improve it until it is satisfactory.

(4) Read the Speaking Performance Assessment Criteria.

(5) Different peer raters rate the transcribed speech separately and repeat the work (when necessary) until the inter-rater reliability is satisfactory (r>.70).

(6) Compare the results and improve the ratings where inconsistencies exist until agreements are reached on all the ratings.

Appendix E Invitation Letter
邀请信

Dear students,

I am seeking your participation in a research concerning a technique on speaking related anxiety, which is hoped to benefit second or foreign language learners. The research is part of the requirement of my study for a Ph. D. degree in Suranaree University of Technology, Thailand. The research involves pre-/posttest of the speaking related anxiety, and speaking performance, or may further involve listening to a lecture. No danger will be involved, though you might experience minutes of nervousness during the test of your speaking performance. All the data collected will only be used by the researcher for the study, and your personal information will be kept confidential.

Participation is voluntary, and withdrawal from the study at any time during the course is at your own choice.

Do you agree to participate? If yes, please put up your hand and let me have your name and means of communication.

Yours truly,
Tianjian Wang

Appendix F　Chinese Script of the Psychoeducation Lecture

1　开场白

　　大家好，欢迎参加演讲。今天演讲的主题是焦虑的根源及其疗法。演讲的目的是促进外语技能发展。首先让我们回顾几件发人深省的事例。

　　2008年3月19日，武汉某高校22岁的一位研究生，被发现跳湖自杀，仅仅因为本科毕业论文涉嫌抄袭。值得吗？为什么会出现如此的悲剧？我们可能难以理解，但对于当事人这是符合逻辑的行为。就在几年前，贵州师范大学某教授发现论文被重庆某高校另一教授抄袭，并起诉该抄袭者赔钱一毛，一时引起轩然大波。但是，这位被指控教授没有自杀，无法在原单位工作，就调动到另一单位继续做教授。为什么？对当事人这是符合逻辑的行为。我有一位侄子，2006年高考差几分不够上重点大学，为了实现重点大学梦想，复读了一年，第二年离重点大学相差几十分。导致这一不可思议结果的主要原因是，第二年高考期间他连续三天反常性失眠，心理压力太大了。有必要么？按照我侄子的逻辑，强大的压力是无法消除的。另外却有很多学生，平时成绩不怎么样，但是遇到重要考试能够泰然自若、正常发挥。为什么？他们的行为也是符合逻辑的。

　　Epictetus，一位Stoic学派哲学家有句著名格言：困扰人们的并不是事物本身，而是他们看待事物的方法。我们可以加上一句，使人们免除苦恼的也是人们看待事物的方法。

　　以上讨论的所有事实和逸闻，都与焦虑的存在或不存在有关。这与当事人看待事物的方式有关。今天我们将讨论与口语相关的焦虑，其基本概念框架适用于以上列举的所有事实。演讲的话题主要包括：

- 焦虑及口语焦虑的概念；
- 口语焦虑与口语的关系；
- 口语焦虑的原因与疗法。

　　演讲设计的原理不仅有助于你们克服有关口语焦虑的心理问题，也有助于克服生活中其他方面的心理问题。

2 背景知识

2.1 口语焦虑的概念

现在我想请各位面对全班作自我介绍。敢说的举手（等候一分钟）。不敢举手的很可能是由于焦虑。焦虑是与目标间接相连的恐惧。与口语相关的焦虑系口语焦虑。如下陈述均为焦虑症状：

- 英语课上，当我知道自己要被老师提问时感到发抖；
- 需要说英语时，我开始感到惊慌；
- 我总觉得其他同学英语说得比我好；
- 在其他同学面前说英语，我觉得害羞、不自然；
- 说英语时我怕违反语法错误。

所有这些陈述均为焦虑的症状（see Horwitz et al., 1991, p.32-33）。

2.2 口语焦虑与口语表达的关系

口语焦虑影响口语表达。研究发现：

- 焦虑者口语表达断断续续，缺乏连贯性；
- 焦虑者口语表达使用过多重复；
- 焦虑者口语表达有大量的句子开头错误；
- 在能力保持一致的情况下，焦虑者口试平均成绩显著低于非焦虑者的成绩。

焦虑影响行为的原理可以通过事例说明。

一位学俄语的泰国朋友说，第一次到莫斯科，总觉得自己的俄语技能欠缺。终于有一天他意外地发现，自己的俄语竟然流利得出乎意料：一位职员惹他生气了，他和职员大吵起来。气得越狠，吵得越凶，吵得越凶，俄语说得越流利。原因很简单，争吵中他没有担忧语法、语音、词汇等细节，减少了思想包袱，因此说得更流利了。

焦虑将注意力分配到与任务有关的思想上（完成任务不可缺少的思维过程，例如沟通中对语言信息的处理），同时也分配到与任务无关的思想上（对完成任务无助的思维，例如沟通中对口音不标准的担忧），认知资源的减少导致了行为效率的下降。另外，焦虑者倾向于回避课堂交谈，这会导致口语技能滞后，引起更严重的焦虑，并形成恶性循环。

口语焦虑具有普遍性。在北京，1/3以上的大学生被发现具有口语焦虑；在江苏，研究发现中学生口语焦虑严重；在台北，调查发现小学生口语焦虑显著。中国颁布的最新大学英语教学目标是发展学生的综合能力，尤其是听说技能。可见口语焦虑直接影响大学英语教学目标核心部分的实现。

3 口语焦虑的根源和疗法

3.1 与目标相关的焦虑及其疗法

（1）目标与焦虑相关

现在假设，你的目标是摘桃子，桃子高度不一，越高越好。如果你强迫自己摘取距离太远的好桃子，你很可能经历焦虑。解决问题的办法之一是改变目标，选择力所能及的对象。跳一跳摘到的桃子是你的最佳选择。

（2）语言学习要循序渐进

现在我们讨论一下语言学习的阶段性。每种语言的学习都是循序渐进的。以母语汉语为例，"我吃饭"是一个简单句子，但是没有人生下来就会说它。在咿呀学语的早期，正常婴儿只能说单词句，例如"饭"。几个月后，方可以说双词句，如"吃饭"。只有到更晚的时候方可以说多词句，如"我吃饭"。强迫新生婴儿说"我吃饭"是脱离实际的。

英语学习遵循同样的顺序。开始你只能说最简单的话，如"hello"；然后你可以说稍难的话，如"nice to meet you"；随后你可以学习更复杂的句子，如"It is so nice for me to see you"。

（3）焦虑者目标脱离实际

焦虑者相信，只有完美的或者最复杂的结构可以使用。他们提前强迫自己去说那些到一定阶段后方可使用的结构，例如"it is nice for me to see you"。如同一个新生婴儿要求自己说"我吃饭"，或者一个人强迫自己摘取过高的桃子。不切实际的目标会导致焦虑。

（4）别小看简单结构

绝不要小看简单结构。一个孤立的词可以组成一个句子，别具很强的交际作用。你到国外后会发现，这些孤立单词多么有用。例如，在餐厅里，如果你口渴了，只用看着服务员，说一个词——"water"，水可能就来了；如果你饿了，说"rice"就可能得到饭；如果要去厕所，说"WC"就可能有人为你指路。日常交际中，不必总是使用标准的时态、语态和语气。

（5）调整目标，满怀信心

为了克服焦虑，请调整你的目标，以适应你目前的水平。能说独词句，就说独词句；能说短语，就说短语；能用复杂结构，就用复杂结构。在不同的发展水平和阶段上，让我们充满同样的信心和勇气。迟早我们会成功掌握一门外语。

3.2 与非理性信念有关的焦虑及其疗法

现在我们讨论第二类导致焦虑的因素："非理性信念"。为了更好理解非理性信念和焦虑的关系，我们需要了解一个基本理论，认识信念是如何影响情绪和行为反应的。

（1）A—B—C 人格理论

现在假设，老师要求你做一次口语演讲。你的信念是：

我非常希望自己的演讲精彩，但这不是必需的。如果演讲不精彩，这当然不是好事，但是天也塌不下来。

如果你有如此信念，你就不会过度焦虑。

现在我们重新假设，老师要求你做一次演讲，你持有如下信念：

我的演讲必须精彩，如果演讲不精彩，那将糟糕至极。

如果你有如此信念，你将经受较强的焦虑。这种焦虑会影响你的演讲。这里的关键之处在于：面对同样的事件，不同的信念导致不同的情绪和行为后果。这就是 A—B—C 人格理论的内涵。

A：事件

B：信念

C：情绪和行为后果

通常人们倾向于认为，A 导致了 C；Ellis 不这样认为，他指出，很多情况下，B 直接导致了 C。

（2）信念引发焦虑案例分析

何种信念导致焦虑？专家指出，我们大部分的焦虑源于僵化极端的信念，或者非理性信念。如下案例分析有助于我们理解非理性信念是如何导致焦虑的。

一位留学生在美国攻读英语博士学位。每次与博导见面时总感到焦虑，因为他认为，与博导说英语时决不能犯错误。他认为犯错误会证明自己是笨蛋。他越这样想，越焦虑，越容易犯错误。让他困扰的问题根源是什么？

根据 A—B—C 人格理论，非理性信念可能是问题的根源。这位学生的第一条信念是，和博导说英语时决不能犯错误。这是非理性的。任何人说任何语言都不能避免语误。这里有一个故事。一位中国的英语学习者曾经在飞机上与一个美国人进行了一次交谈。

"What's your wife?" 中国人问。

"She do not work." 美国人回答。

"She do not work?" 中国人吃惊地重复。

"No, she do not." 美国人漫不经心地回答。

正确的说法是"does not"，而不是"do not"。这位中国人原以为本族人的英语完美无缺，因此对其语法错误感到惊讶。而这位美国人毫不在乎，因为这是正常现象。不信么？你可以对朋友的母语谈话进行录音，然后交给语言专家分析，你就会发现语误多么频繁。语误是如此频繁，以至于我们已经对其失去了敏感性。

在上述的案例中，那位学生僵化地要求自己决不能犯语言错误是非理性的，这导致了他的焦虑。

这位学生的第二条信念是，犯错误会证明他笨蛋，这也是非理性的。一个人的智力包括很多方面。根据 Gardner（1983）的理论，人有 7 种智力（见下表）。

智力类型	功能
Linguistic	words and language
Logical-Mathematical	logic and numbers
Musical	music, sound, rhythm
Bodily-Kinesthetic	body movement control
Spatial-Visual	images and space
Interpersonal	other people's feelings
Intrapersonal	self-awareness

案例中的学生仅仅抽取口语表达贬低整个自我，犯了以偏概全的逻辑错误。这一非理性信念是他焦虑的另一根源。

如何治疗他的烦恼？由于焦虑源于非理性信念，使用理性信念替换非理性信念有望控制或降低焦虑。如果这位学生的信念替换为"与导师说英语时，我希望不犯错误。但这不是必须达到的。语误不会证明我是笨蛋。它只能证明我是一个会犯错误的人，而且是这一次犯了语误"，他还会有强焦虑吗？不大可能。

（3）课堂口语表达相关的非理性与理性信念

根据 Dryden（2001）的理性情绪疗法理论，在第二语言教室中，有四类非理性信念：僵化的要求、灾难化信念、挫折低容忍信念、自我贬低的信念，其中讲话的要求是核心成分。与非理性信念对应，有4类理性信念：热切的希望、反灾难化信念、挫折高容忍信念和自我接纳的信念，其中热切的希望是核心成分。如下部分将成对讨论非理性与理性信念。

A. 僵化的要求与热切的希望

僵化的要求是一种认为事情必须如何或者决不能如何的僵化信念（Dryden，2001，p.4）。例如：

- "我说英语时必须遵守语法规则"；
- "我的发音必须准确"；
- "我必须完美地回答问题"；
- "我的英语老师必须给我肯定性评价"；
- "决不能让朋友嘲笑我的口语"。

根据 Dryden（2001）的观点，诸如此类的僵化要求都是非理性的，是我们许多口语焦虑的核心。

热切的希望是一种希望事情如何而不强求其必须如何的灵活信念。例如：

- "我希望说英语时遵守语法规则，但这不是必须的"；
- "我希望自己的发音准确，但这不是必须的"；
- "我希望完美地回答问题，但回答也可以是不完美的"；
- "我希望英语老师给我肯定性评价，但不幸的是，他未必这样"；
- "我希望朋友不嘲笑我的口语，不幸的是，他们也可以嘲笑我"。

根据 Dryden（2001）的观点，诸如此类的热切的希望是理性的，是对口语行为产生健康心理反应的核心。

热切的希望为何是理性的？热切的希望具有两个外显成分："希望"以及"对僵化要求的否定"，两部分均具有灵活性。例如：

我希望表达正确（"希望"：灵活），但这不是必须的（"对僵化要求的否定"的否定：灵活）。

之所以说热切的希望是理性的，是因为灵活的"希望"成分可以合理地推导出灵活的"对僵化要求的否定"。

僵化的要求为何是非理性的？僵化的要求看起来似乎只有一个成分，但事实上它有两个成分，另一个被暗含其中。例如，当你说你必须立即吃午饭，别人可以合理地推导出你希望立即吃午饭。僵化的要求的两个成分分别为"希望"和"僵化的要求"，前者灵活，后者不灵活。例如：

我希望表达正确（"希望"：灵活），所以我必须表达正确（"僵化的要求"：不灵活）。

僵化的要求之所以是非理性的，是因为灵活的"希望"不能够合理地推导出不灵活的"僵化的要求"。

僵化的要求对学习有害。这些信念脱离实际。这种信念持有者课堂上会经历较强焦虑，因为他们能够意识到可能出现的挫折。为了避免挫折发生，他们会通过逃课、拒绝主动发言等方式，设法避免在群体中讲话。最终结果是外语学习的失败。

热切的希望有益。一方面，热切的希望能够为学习者提供足够的动力向着追求的目标迈进；另一方面，学习者不会遭受挫折的威胁。热切的希望可以导致心平气和、大胆参与、积极尝试，最终结果是学习成功。

B. 灾难化信念与反灾难化信念

灾难化信念是僵化的要求得不到满足时的衍生物之一。这些信念是非理性的（Dryden，2001，p. 5）。例如：

- "我说英语时必须遵守语法规则，否则糟糕至极"；
- "我的发音必须准确，否则太可怕了"；
- "我必须完美地回答问题，否则简直是世界末日"；
- "我的英语老师必须给我肯定性评价，否则后果不堪设想"；
- "决不能让朋友嘲笑我的口语，否则太骇人了"。

灾难化信念是非理性的。灾难化信念具有极端性。这种信念持有者当时具有如下一种或两种看法：

☐ 没有比此事更糟糕的了（Dryden，2001，p. 5）；

☐ 从这件坏事中得不到任何益处（Dryden，2001，p. 5）。

两种看法都是非理性的。妈妈曾经告诉儿子：从他出生的那一刻起，到他躺到灵柩内为止，世界上不存在任何事情不能变得更坏（Nie，2009，p73）。持有灾难化信念的学习者倾向于夸张后果的严重性：一切不受欢迎的（不可取的、不合意的、不愉快的、不完美的……）都是可怕的

（骇人的、糟糕的、灾难化的……）。按照辩证法，对待坏事的绝对化看法也是非理性的。在外语学习中，我们能够从不完美的表达行为中受益。专家们把不完美的第二语言称为中介语，它既不同于母语，也不同于目标语。正常情况下，第二语言学习者会逐渐完善中介语，直到它与目标语一样。你在表达中不完美的行为反映了你正在正常发展。就连别人对你产生的否定性反应对你也有益处，因为这可以帮你意识到自己的欠缺之处。

灾难化信念的健康替代物为反灾难化信念。反灾难化信念是非极端化的信念，它是热切的希望得不到满足时的衍生物之一（Dryden，2001，p. 5）。它是理性的。例如：

- "我希望说英语时遵守语法规则，但这不是必须的。犯语法错误虽然有失完美，但也并不可怕"；
- "我希望自己的发音准确，但这不是必须的，发音不标准虽然不可取，但也没什么大不了的"；
- "我希望完美地回答问题，但回答也可以是不完美的，不完美的回答不理想，但也不是世界末日"；
- "我希望英语老师给我肯定性评价，但不幸的是，他未必这样。如果他没有给我肯定性评价，的确让人遗憾，但这并不可怕"；
- "我希望朋友不嘲笑我的口语，不幸的是，他们也可以嘲笑我。如果他们嘲笑了，的确让人遗憾，但这没有什么大不了的"。

反灾难化信念是理性的，是非极端的。信念持有者当时怀有如下一种或多种看法：

□ 这并不是极端糟糕的事（Dryden，2001，p. 5）；
□ 这件坏事也可以让人受益（Dryden，2001，p. 5）。

两种看法均属于理性看法，因为它们与灾难化信念持有者的非理性观点形成鲜明对比。

在语言教室中，灾难化信念对学习有害。持有这种信念的学习者会经历过强的焦虑，因为他们会感觉到种种"灾难"的存在。为了避免"灾难"的发生，这些学习者会想方设法地回避在群体中开口，这最终会导致学习的失败。反灾难化信念有益，这种信念持有者眼中没有什么"灾难"，因此没有相应的焦虑。他们更有可能参与课堂互动，大胆进行口语尝试，最终取得学习成功。

C. 挫折低容忍信念和挫折高容忍信念

挫折低容忍信念是极端化的信念，是僵化的要求得不到满足时的衍生物之一（Dryden，2001，p. 6）。这种信念是非理性的。例如：
- "我说英语时必须遵守语法规则，否则我将无法忍受"；
- "我的发音必须准确，否则令人难受"；
- "我必须完美地回答问题，否则我自己都无法忍耐"；
- "我的英语老师必须给我肯定性评价，否则我承受不了"；
- "决不能让朋友嘲笑我的口语，否则我接受不了"。

挫折低容忍信念是非理性的。挫折低容忍信念具有极端性。信念持有者当时相信如下一种或多种看法：

□ 如果这种挫折或者不舒服的现象继续存在，我将死亡或者崩溃（Dryden，2001，p. 6）；

□ 如果这种挫折或者不舒服的现象继续存在，我将失去体验幸福和快乐的能力（Dryden，2001，p. 6）。

两种观念都是非理性的。在第二语言学习中，很少有过关于某位学生因为不完美的表达，或者别人对其不完美的表达产生的否定性反应，而死亡、精神崩溃或者失去体验幸福的能力的报道。即使一个人声称他/她不能忍受某件事，一旦事情发生了他/她事实上已经在忍受着这件事。挫折低容忍信念持有者倾向于认为一切难以忍受的、一切不舒服不愉快的现象都属于不能够忍受的。

挫折低容忍信念的健康替代物是挫折高容忍信念。挫折高容忍信念是非极端的信念，是热切的希望得不到满足时产生的衍生物之一（Dryden，2001，p. 6）。它们是理性的。例如：
- "我希望说英语时遵守语法规则，但这不是必须的。犯语法错误让人忍受起来不舒服，但我能够忍受，并且它值得我忍受"；
- "我希望自己的发音准确，但这不是必须的。发音不标准让人忍受起来虽然别扭，但我能够忍受，我这样做也是值得的"；
- "我希望完美地回答问题，但回答也可以是不完美的。不完美的回答让人不太好受，但我能够忍受，我可以从容忍中受益"；
- "我希望英语老师给我肯定性评价，但不幸的是，他未必这样。如果他没有给我肯定性评价，的确让人不好接受，但我可以接受它，而且接受对我有益"；
- "我希望朋友不嘲笑我的口语，不幸的是，他们也可以嘲笑我。

如果他们嘲笑了，的确让人不好忍受，但我能够忍受，忍一忍对我有好处"。

挫折高容忍信念是理性的，是非极端的。信念持有者当时怀有如下一种或多种看法：

- 如果这种挫折或者不舒服的现象继续存在，我将继续努力，但我既不会死亡也不会崩溃（Dryden，2001，p.6）；
- 如果这种挫折或者不舒服的现象继续存在，我将不会失去体验幸福和快乐的能力，尽管我暂时体验不到幸福和快乐（Dryden，2001，p.6）。
- 这种挫折或者不舒服的现象值得忍受（Dryden，2001，p.6）。

所有这些观念都是理性的，因为它们与挫折低容忍信念持有者的非理性观念形成鲜明的对比。挫折高容忍信念并不意味着不去尝试改变现实。相反，它意味着学习者将逐渐完善个人的行为，同时又不受暂时非完美行为的困扰。另外，不完美的行为也值得忍受，因为学习者可以从中获得某种益处。

挫折低容忍信念对学习有害。如果学习者认为他们不能够容忍不完美的口语表达或者别人对他们表达的否定性评价（其中某些可能只是个人错觉），他们会经历较强的焦虑，因为这些事件在语言课堂上难以避免。学习者会通过各种办法避免这些事件的发生，如逃课、拒绝参与课堂互动或者举手发言。这些行为最终会导致语言学习的失败。挫折高容忍信念会带来心平气和、积极的课堂参与和最终的学习成功。如同一个驾驶员通过参照外部环境能够保持正确的驶向，不管来自别人的反馈是肯定性的还是否定性的，都有助于个人更加有效地掌握语言。

D. 自我贬低的信念与自我接纳的信念

自我贬低的信念是关于个人的极端化观念，是僵化的要求不能得到满足时的衍生物之一（Dryden，2001）。例如：

- "我说英语时必须遵守语法规则，否则会证明我是一个笨蛋"；
- "我的发音必须准确，否则将意味着我的语言天赋低"；
- "我必须完美地回答问题，否则将意味着我是一个很差劲的学生"；
- "我必须得到英语老师的肯定性评价，否则就意味着我没有价值"；

- "决不能让朋友嘲笑我的口语，否则会证明我是一个傻瓜"。

自我贬低的信念是非理性的，具有极端性。信念持有者当时怀有如下一种或者几种看法：

- 给一个人贴上一个单独的标签，以界定一个人的本质是合理的，并且个人的价值取决于变化不定的情景（Dryden, 2001, p. 7）（例如：表现好的时候我的价值上升，表现差的时候我的价值下降）；
- 根据个人的孤立的方面来评价整个人是合理的（Dryden, 2001, p. 7）。

自我贬低的信念是非理性的。首先，每个人都是一个复杂的整体，包含方方面面的特征。如果我们用小些字母"i"代表自我的一部分，大写"I"代表整个自我，那么大写"I"包含许多小写"i"，但任何一个小写"i"都不等于大写"I"。大写"I"不能通过某个小写"i"来鉴定（见下图）。

$$i \neq I$$

其次，个人的表现行为受到许多情景因素的影响，但是一个人的价值是稳定的。稳定的价值不能通过变化不定的行为来评价。自我贬低的信念是荒谬的，因为它依据部分自我界定整个自我，依据变化不定的情景评价稳定的个人本质。例如，"如果我在一件事情上表现不好，我将在所有事情上表现不好"，或者说"如果我这一次表现不完美，我将永远表现不完美"。

自我贬低信念的健康替代物为自我接纳的信念。自我接纳的信念是关于个人的非极端的信念，是热切的希望得不到满足时的衍生物之一。它们是理性的（Dryden, 2001）。例如：

- "我希望说英语时遵循语法规则，但这不是必须的。如果没有遵循语法规则，这并不能证明我是一个笨蛋，我只是一个和别人一样的人，在口语表达中有时会犯语法错误"；
- "我希望自己的发音准确，但这不是必须的，如果我的发音不标准，这并不意味着我的语言天赋低，它仅仅意味着在目前的发展阶段，我的语音还没有达到尽善尽美的程度"；

- "我希望完美地回答问题，但回答也可以是不完美的，回答不完美并不能说明我就是一个很差劲的学生，我只不过和别人一样，有时候回答问题是不完美的"；
- "我希望得到英语老师的肯定性评价，但这不是必须的。如果他没有给我肯定性评价，这并不意味着我没有价值可言，因为我也有受到老师肯定性评价的时候"；
- "我希望朋友不嘲笑我的口语，不幸的是，他们也可以嘲笑我，如果他们嘲笑了，这并不表明我是一个傻瓜，因为我也有受到他们钦佩的时候"。

自我接纳的信念是理性的，是非极端的。信念持有者当时怀有如下一种或者多种看法：

- 不能给一个人贴上一个单独的标签，以界定一个人的本质，并且个人的价值并不取决于变化不定的情景（Dryden，2001，p.7）（例如：不管我表现如何，我的个人价值保持不变）；
- 评价个人的孤立方面未尝不可，但根据个人的孤立的方面来评价整个人就没有意义了（Dryden，2001）。

自我接纳的信念是理性的，因为它与自我贬低信念持有者的非理性观点正好相反。

自我贬低信念对学习有害。在语言教室里，口语表达很少是至善至美的，来自别人的消极反应也可能存在（其中某些属于个人错觉）。自我贬低信念持有者将经历过强焦虑，因为在他们的知觉中，个人价值随时有可能受到威胁。为了保护个人价值，这些学习者会采取各种方法回避课堂交流，这最终会导致语言学习的失败。自我接纳的信念，正好与此相反，可以带来心平气和的情绪，参与课堂互动的积极性，以及最终的学习成功。

4 收场白

既然对口语焦虑有了完整的理解，下一步就是要控制口语焦虑，改变破坏性的课堂行为。你需要为自己的表达选择适当的目标或者标准：如果你能够使用孤立的单词，就说这些单词；如果你能够使用短语，就说短语；如果你能够使用简单句子，就说简单句子；如果你能够使用复杂句子，就说复杂句子。开口有益。理智的选择是：希望自己的表达完美，但不要僵化地自我要求。不要担忧不完美的表达，告诉自己要容忍暂时的美中不足。不要因为不完美的表达行为自我贬低。

在外语课堂上，设立你的情绪目标，诸如"我将放松、舒服、愉快"等；设定你的行为目标，诸如"我将充分利用机会说英语，我将举手发言"等等。你的行为目标应该逐渐变大。例如，第一周，你可以让自己在课堂上举手发言一次；第二周两次，以此类推。最初，你可以在有准备的情况下试图回答问题，随后在毫无准备的情况下尝试。再后来，面对全班。当你能够在班上舒服地表达的时候，尝试在其他陌生、正式的场合，诸如口语赛上等表达。同时，定期思考和评价个人的进步。如果你对个人进步自我满意，进行自我强化，强化方式可以是美食品尝，公园漫步，景点观光等等。长期下去，你会从这些尝试中受益匪浅。

演讲到此结束！谢谢大家！

Appendix G   Distribution of Selections on the Likert Scales

(The selection refers to: of all the participants responding to the scale, the percentage of selections on a choice following an item)

Table 1   Selections on the Speaking Anxiety Scale (Research Question 1)

Item	Selection (%)				
	Strongly agree	Agree	Undecided	Disagree	Strongly disagree
1	10.8	26.7	17.9	36.3	8.3
2	3.8	25.0	23.8	39.2	8.2
3	10.8	33.8	18.3	35.0	2.1
4	12.9	48.8	17.1	16.7	4.5
5	8.8	34.6	20.4	29.6	6.6
6	3.8	22.1	35.4	31.3	7.4
7	8.8	42.9	20.0	26.3	2.0
8	9.2	30.0	16.3	40.0	4.5
9	1.7	20.8	31.3	37.9	8.3
10	8.8	28.3	15.0	42.1	5.8
11	1.7	27.5	21.3	42.1	7.4
12	1.3	11.3	29.2	47.9	10.3
13	4.2	19.6	16.3	49.6	10.3
14	2.1	20.0	14.6	52.1	11.2
15	2.9	14.6	33.3	37.9	11.3

Table 2   Selections on Trait Anxiety Scale (Research Question 2)

	Item	Selection (%)			
		Not at all	Somewhat	Moderately so	Very much so
TA	1	1.9	16.5	60.2	21.4
	2	16.5	32.0	46.6	4.9
	3	7.8	17.5	61.2	13.5
	4	3.9	24.3	53.4	18.4
	5	2.9	18.4	49.5	29.2
	6	23.3	52.4	18.4	5.9
	7	6.8	23.3	49.5	20.4
	8	11.7	32.0	42.7	13.6
	9	13.6	38.8	38.8	8.8
	10	5.8	30.1	49.5	14.6

Table 3　　　**Selections on Unwillingness to Communicate Scale (Research Question 2)**

	Item	Strongly agree	Agree	Undecided	Disagree	Strongly disagree
UTC	1	3.9	19.4	32.0	37.9	6.8
	2	1.0	7.8	25.2	43.7	22.3
	3	4.9	25.2	25.2	39.8	4.9
	4	9.7	35.0	40.8	13.5	1.0
	5	1.0	25.2	19.4	42.7	11.7
	6	10.7	35.9	34.0	19.4	0.0
	7	0.0	23.3	23.3	40.8	12.6
	8	0.0	7.8	21.4	57.3	13.5
	9	1.0	7.8	22.3	63.1	5.8
	10	5.8	26.2	33.0	30.1	4.9
	11	0.0	4.9	21.4	63.1	10.6
	12	0.0	4.9	21.4	55.3	18.4
	13	10.7	64.1	22.3	2.9	0.0
	14	1.0	9.7	18.4	56.3	14.6
	15	12.6	43.7	32.0	11.7	0.0
	16	0.0	18.4	18.4	47.6	15.6
	17	6.8	61.2	28.2	3.8	0.0
	18	8.7	74.8	13.6	2.9	0.0
	19	0.0	1.0	19.4	59.2	20.4
	20	0.0	1.0	3.9	51.5	43.6

Table 4   Selections on Speaking Anxiety Scale
(Research Question 2)

	Item	Strongly agree	Agree	Undecided	Disagree	Strongly disagree
SA	1	4.9	24.3	15.5	45.6	9.7
	2	1.0	22.3	20.4	45.6	10.7
	3	11.7	35.0	17.5	35.8	
	4	7.8	49.5	21.4	14.6	6.7
	5	6.8	35.9	18.4	33.0	5.9
	6	3.9	26.2	37.9	30.1	1.9
	7	6.8	44.7	18.4	27.2	2.9
	8	6.8	30.1	13.6	44.7	4.8
	9	1.0	24.2	36.9	36.9	1.0
	10	2.9	22.3	10.7	57.3	6.8
	11		24.3	22.3	46.6	6.8
	12	2.9	13.6	33.0	44.7	5.8
	13	2.9	19.4	11.7	56.3	9.7
	14	2.9	17.5	16.5	54.4	8.7
	15	1.0	19.4	35.9	35.9	7.8

Table 5   Language Class Risk-Taking/Sociability Scale
(Research Question 2)

	Item	Strongly agree	Agree	Undecided	Disagree	Strongly disagree
LCR (1-6) and LCS (7-11)	1	6.8	23.3	12.6	44.7	12.6
	2	6.8	40.8	18.4	28.2	5.8
	3	8.7	54.4	14.6	19.4	2.9
	4	6.8	43.7	17.5	29.1	2.9
	5	13.6	63.0	11.7	11.7	
	6	5.8	46.6	16.5	30.1	1.0
	7	13.6	44.7	29.1	11.6	1.0
	8	1.9	14.6	44.7	36.9	1.9
	9	2.9	29.1	35.9	31.1	1.0
	10	24.3	56.3	15.5	3.9	
	11	43.7	47.6	7.7	1.0	

Table 6   Selections on Speaking Self-Efficacy Scale
(Research Question 2)

	Item	Selection (%)					
		1	2	3	4	5	missing
SSE	1	5.8	21.4	48.5	22.3	2.0	
	2	3.9	13.6	39.8	34.0	8.7	
	3	7.8	21.4	48.5	17.5	3.8	1.0
	4	2.9	9.7	35.0	35.9	15.5	1.0
	5	18.4	35.9	36.9	7.8		1.0
	6	8.7	27.2	29.1	24.3	9.7	1.0
	7	3.9	35.9	48.5	11.7		

Table 7   Selections on the Speaking Anxiety Scale
(Research Question 3-4)

	Item	Test	Selection (%)				
			Strongly agree	Agree	Undecided	Disagree	Strongly disagree
SA	1	pre	6.3	12.5	12.5	59.4	9.3
		post	3.1	18.8	12.5	59.4	6.2
	2	pre	3.1	25.0	21.9	43.8	6.2
		post		15.6	18.8	56.3	9.3
	3	pre	6.2	34.4	9.4	43.8	6.2
		post	3.1	43.8	21.9	31.2	
	4	pre	6.3	40.6	21.9	25.0	6.2
		post		37.5	21.9	40.6	
	5	pre	6.3	31.3	15.6	40.6	6.2
		post	3.1	18.8	21.9	50.0	6.2
	6	pre		43.8	25.0	25.0	6.2
		post		25.0	53.1	15.6	6.3
	7	pre	9.4	21.9	31.3	34.4	3.0
		post	3.1	21.9	25.0	43.8	6.2
	8	pre	3.1	25.0	18.8	50.0	3.1
		post		21.9	15.6	56.3	6.2

	Item	Test	Selection (%)				
			Strongly agree	Agree	Undecided	Disagree	Strongly disagree
SA	9	pre	3.1	37.5	31.3	21.9	6.2
		post		31.3	46.9	18.8	3.0
	10	pre	3.1	25.0	6.3	53.1	12.5
		post		28.1	6.3	56.3	9.3
	11	pre	9.4	15.6	18.8	46.9	9.3
		post		21.9	15.6	53.1	9.4
	12	pre		34.4	18.8	40.6	6.2
		post		25.0	34.4	37.5	3.1
	13	pre		25.0	9.4	59.4	6.2
		post		21.9	9.4	62.5	6.2
	14	pre		15.6	12.5	59.4	12.5
		post		15.6	21.9	62.5	
	15	pre	12.5	12.5	31.3	34.4	9.3
		post	3.1	12.5	46.9	34.4	3.1

Table 8   Selections on Speaking State Anxiety Scale
(Research Question 3-4)

	Item	Test	Selection (%)				
			Strongly agree	Agree	Undecided	Disagree	Strongly disagree
SAstate	1	Pre	6.3	62.5	25.0	6.2	
		Post	6.3	56.3	18.7	18.7	
	2	Pre	3.1	59.4	6.3	31.2	
		Post	3.1	46.9	9.4	40.6	
	3	Pre	3.1	18.8	15.6	56.3	6.2
		Post		12.5	25.0	59.4	3.1
	4	Pre		40.6	15.6	40.6	3.2
		Post		31.3	15.6	50	3.1

continued

	Item	Test	Selection (%)			
			Strongly agree	Agree	Undecided	Disagree	Strongly disagree
SAstate	5	Pre	3.1	68.8	15.6	12.5	
		Post	6.3	62.5	12.5	18.7	
	6	Pre		50.0	9.4	40.6	
		Post		34.4	31.3	34.3	
	7	Pre		34.4	18.8	46.8	
		Post		28.1	18.8	53.1	
	8	Pre	9.4	62.5	12.5	15.6	
		Post	3.1	56.3	21.9	18.7	